READING DRAWINGS

an introduction to looking at drawings

Susan Lambert

Pantheon Books New York

Published in Great Britain as *Drawing: Technique and Purpose* by Trefoil Books Ltd.

Library of Congress Cataloging in Publication Data

Lambert, Susan.
  Reading drawings.

    1. Drawing — Themes, motives. 2. Picture perception.
I. Title.
NC715.L35 1984   741'.01'1   83-23824

ISBN 0-394-72479-8 (pbk.)

An earlier version of the text first issued to accompany the exhibition "Drawing: Technique and Purpose" in London in 1981.

Published on the occasion of the exhibition "Reading Drawings" at the Drawing Center (a nonprofit space for the study and exhibition of drawings), 137 Greene Street, New York, N.Y. 10012, in April 1984.

Designed by Rupert Kirby
Color photography by Prudence Cuming
Set in Plantin Light by Words & Pictures Ltd.
Printed and bound by Jolly & Barber Ltd., Rugby, England
Manufactured in Great Britain

First American Edition

CONTENTS

Cover illustration: *see* fig. 20.
Title page illustration: *see* fig. 35.

It is with pride that the Drawing Center presents this exhibition in celebration of its seventh anniversary. The Center is a nonprofit institution, founded in 1977, that seeks through exhibition and education to express the quality and diversity of drawing – unique works on paper – as a major art form. Each year the Center presents at least five exhibitions. Those of an historical nature such as *Reading Drawings* complement its program of showing drawings by contemporary artists whose work is not yet represented by commercial galleries and is not ordinarily on view in New York. It is particularly important for the Drawing Center to present this exhibition from the Victoria & Albert Museum, London, stressing both how and why drawings are made. This book and the exhibition it accompanies underscore the importance of drawing to Western culture over the past five centuries. I would like to thank C.M. Kauffmann, Keeper of the Department of Prints, Drawings & Photographs, and Paintings at the Victoria & Albert Museum for kindly agreeing to lend us this exhibition. I am also deeply grateful to Susan Lambert, Deputy Keeper, for her brilliant organization of the exhibition and original and informative catalog essay. Their graciousness and generosity have made this event a great pleasure. I also want to thank our publisher, Conway Lloyd Morgan, who has continually solved problems with goodwill and good cheer.

The organization of this exhibition was greatly facilitated by the constant support of the Directors of the Drawing Center. Special thanks go to my colleagues Jane Fluegel, Director of Development, William Irvine, Administrative Assistant, and Marie Keller, Associate Curator. All of us thank the many work/study students and interns who have made our tasks easier and more pleasurable.

Finally, I would like to thank the following people who have helped in innumerable ways:

Mrs. Vincent Astor, Huntington T. Block, Geoff Bridges, Mr. and Mrs. Michael Coles, Keith Davis, Monika Dillon, Thomas Freudenheim, Linda Gillies, Peter Gilmore, George de Gramont, Sydney Gruson, Michael Iovenko, Antoinette King, Michael Lapetina, Peter Laundy, Thomas Lawson, Mary Mancuso, Donald B. Marron, Colin Marshall, Ward Mintz, George Negroponte, Andrew Oliver, Thomas Rhoads, Gilbert Robinson, Steven Rogers, Sarah Rubenstein, Samuel Sachs II, André Schiffrin, Ray Smyth, Leslie Spector, Harry Taylor, Brenda Trimarco, Massimo Vignelli, James D. Wolfensohn.

Martha Beck, Director, The Drawing Center

FOREWORD

This book has its origins in an exhibition held at the Victoria & Albert Museum in 1981. It marked the centenary of exhibitions of Old Master drawings, for, leaving aside earlier isolated examples, a convenient point of departure for a modern history of such exhibitions would be the show of *Zeichnungen Alter Meister* in the Berlin Print Room in 1881. They have increased immeasurably in number and scale since the Second World War and the success of recent exhibitions of drawings, by, for example, Raphael, Leonardo and Claude, has demonstrated the wide popularity of what was once thought to be a minority taste.

Yet these exhibitions, as, indeed, most books on Old Master drawings, have been devoted to individual artists, schools or collections. There is no readily available book which attempts to show both how and why drawings are made, and it is with these two questions that Susan Lambert's book deals. But whereas the question of technique can be readily treated, that of purpose is not always easy to define. The three types discussed here: *drawing as a discipline*, *drawing as imagination*, and *drawing for utility* should be seen as suitable starting points for an enquiry rather than as immutable categories. What the book does demonstrate beyond any doubt is the central importance of drawing to generations of artists and to all the visual arts.

The Victoria & Albert Museum's collection is ideal for the purpose of illustrating these themes. Unlike most Print Rooms, which collect drawings to represent schools and styles, the Victoria & Albert has always been more concerned with the purpose for which drawings are made. Consequently it contains large collections of academic drawings made in the process of educating artists, of designs for illustration and, in particular, of drawings used at the various preparatory stages in the production of paintings, sculpture, architecture and the applied arts. But this, it must be stressed, is not to belittle their intrinsic quality, and it is hoped that the reader will agree that many of the works discussed in this book are among the finest drawings ever produced.

C.M. Kauffmann
Keeper, Dept. of Prints, Drawings & Photographs,
and Paintings
Victoria & Albert Museum

Detail of Plate III. Jacopo Tintoretto
(1518-1594); Italian
A kneeling monk
Inscribed *G. Tintoretto* in an eighteenth-
century hand, with the collector's mark of
Sir Joshua Reynolds (Lugt. 234)
Black chalk heightened with white on blue
integrally coloured laid paper, squared for
transfer. 35.5 x 24.2 cm.
The figure may be a study for the kneeling
apostle in the 'Assumption of the Virgin' in
the Accademia, Venice. Drawing on mid-
toned paper enabled the painter to design in
much the same way as in chiaroscuro
painting. The all-pervading tone of the
paper linked both light and dark colours laid
on it, increasing the effect of unity.
Bibl: Ward-Jackson I 329.

INTRODUCTION

Artists and writers on art, from Cennino Cennini in the fourteenth century, to Klee in the twentieth, have stressed the importance of drawing, some considering it the most basic skill of both the artist and the designer. But what is a drawing? The term, often surrounded by confusion, is difficult to define. Not surprisingly, different groups during different periods have understood it in different ways, since the Renaissance when the term *disegno* implied drawing both as a technique to be distinguished from colouring and also as the creative idea made visible in the preliminary sketch. To drawing there has also been attached a certain mystique deriving from a belief that the creativity of the artist re-enacted the creation of the world. According to Leonardo da Vinci, for example, *disegno* was not only a science but a deity, whose name was worthy of commemoration, because it offered a replica of all the visible works of God the highest.

This reverence for drawing was reiterated in many drawing manuals. For example W. Gore, in his editon of Gerhard of Brugge's *An introduction to the general art of drawing*, published in 1674, claimed that: 'The art of drawing... may justly be called a bearing mother of all arts and sciences whatever, for whatsoever is made begets thorow the same a good aspect and well-being; and besides all this, the art of drawing is the beginning and end, or finisher of all things imaginable, wherefore she may be called a sense of poesie, a second nature, a living book of all things past. She is called a poesie, because that she, thorow falshoods and masked faces, represents unto the beholder the truth of things present and past, and by pleasant resemblances makes us in a manner believe to see that, which indeed we see not. A second nature she is called, because she teacheth thorow drawings, to imitate and to set forth all the works of the Creation. A living book she is called, of things present and past; because that she brings into remembrance to the beholder of her, things long since past, so that at sight, or the least aspect of any praiseworthy history (in our minde, and in our understanding) we receive a profitable exercise, a fair invitation to imitate their laudable acts, and a pleasure in beholding; and more than this, she brings to remembrance the deeds of people and nations, dead long since; and the features and resemblance of our fathers, grandfathers, and great-grand-fathers, she represents as living in dead shades long after their time.' [1]

Much of the magic of drawing lies in its inherently subjective nature. For drawn marks provide parallels with experience. Swelling or tapering, straight or curved lines, dots and dashes, diagonal, vertical and horizontal hatching and tonal shading are able to suggest form, space, light and movement without having any true similarity to the subjects they describe. Dictionary definitions do not always take into account this element of superficial deceit. The *Shorter Oxford Dictionary* offers a definition of 'drawing' with which many would agree: 'the formation of a line by drawing some tracing instrument from point to point of a surface; representation by lines; delineation as distinguished from painting...the arrangment of the lines which determine form...' But despite this insistence on the linear, few would deny that Seurat's dotted tonal works in chalk are drawings (fig. 64), and those who argue that drawings are primarily monochrome would probably agree that, for example, the brush sketch executed in yellow, brown and purple by Procaccini reproduced as plate V is, nevertheless, a drawing.

For our purpose we have interpreted 'drawing' as widely as possible, bringing together an immense variety of examples from different countries and periods; it is only with regret that we decided to limit ourselves to works made in the West. For those interested in a particular aspect, such very breadth of scope will inevitably emphasize the gaps. It is our hope that the selection is rich enough to provide each reader with at least a few drawings which will give intense pleasure and many others which will reward close study. The prime reason for this publication is not, however, to reproduce a treasury of master drawings. The aim is to look at the materials with which drawings are made and to explore some of the reasons why drawings have been made. Although the aesthetic quality of a particular drawing may seem reason enough for its existence, they often owe their existence to utilitarian considerations. In fact, in terms of sheer numbers most drawings are practical: thousands may be made during the production of a new car design, for example.

Here the reader will not find drawings discussed by *genera* such as landscape or portrait, nor in chronological order nor by country, but in four main categories embracing all subjects, eras and schools. Many attempts have been made to divide drawings into clearly defined categories but the results are inevitably somewhat arbitrary. Our own choice – technique, drawing as a discipline, drawing as imagination and drawing for utility – is no exception. There is nothing exclusive or rigid about these categories. Moreoever, within each of the main categories there are many subdivisions, divergences and special cases.

Some of the drawings could have been placed appropriately under any of the main headings. The reason why a drawing has been made is often not clear, partly because a single drawing can have many functions both for the artist who made it and for his public. What starts as a doodle may turn out to contain the germ of an idea for a major work, or what begins as an exercise such as copying from nature may result in a form which the artist will incorporate into some subsequent and unrelated composition. It is often quoted that Delacroix 'loosened up' his hand by drawing from his imagination before he began painting, but sketches made in this way provided him with a bank of ideas which could be dipped into later. A portrait may be drawn solely as an exercise (a number of artists are known to have used their own features in this way).

Equally a portrait drawing may be made prepartory to a painting or as an end in itself. If the latter is the case, two ideas are at work, the artist's interpretation of the sitter and his struggle to make an accurate record of the person portrayed, and distinguishing between these two may be difficult if not impossible.

The situation is further complicated by the application of our categories across ten centuries during which attitudes to drawing have altered considerably. With time, some of the functions of drawing have been superseded by mechanical or technical developments. Until the invention of printmaking in the fifteenth century, copying by hand was the only means of multiplying an image. So illustrations in manuscripts played the same part as printed illustrations in books do to-day, but a system of classification should distinguish such works from drawings made for reproduction in another medium. Likewise the purpose of making drawings to record information has been subtly changed by the invention of photography: photographs provide excellent records of a kind, but drawing allows, for example, the subject to be separated from its natural habitat or for selected details to be emphasized.

The framework we have adopted for presenting our subject inevitably creates some apparently bizarre juxtapositions. But these are not unintentional: we hope that an approach that relates drawing to artistic purpose, rather than relegating it to connoisseurship will go some way to suggest the central part drawing has played and still plays in the development of ideas in Western art and, by extension, in our civilization.

TECHNIQUE

1. Probably by Bernardo Parentino
(1437-1531); Italian
Venus and Cupid trampling on a Serpent
Inscribed in ink *M.I.* (Lugt 2981) and
Antonio Poll
Pen and ink on vellum. 24.2 x 17.1 cm.(detail)
Ink on vellum was well adapted to express,
through hatching, the clarity of quattrocento
painting. Very similar hatching was used in
contemporary Italian engravings, and it has
been suggested that this drawing is preparatory to such a print. The mount with its wash
lines is of the type which were attached to
drawings from the collection of Padre Resta
(1635-1714) on their acquisition by Lord
Somers (1650-1716).
Bibl: Ward-Jackson I 14. *See* Plate I.

Facing page: Fra Bartolommeo, detail of
Plate II

'Because of its particular appearance and its necessary manner of handling, every material is pervaded by a unique spirit and poetry, which in the hands of the artist greatly strengthens the character of the representation, and for which there is no substitute – in much the same way that the character of a piece of music depends upon its predetermined key.' [2] This thought, expressed by the German painter, etcher and sculptor, Max Klinger (1857-1920), applies to the different materials used in drawing. The drawings in this chapter have been selected with a view to examining their physical make-up and to bringing out some of the different expressive qualities which result from the use of various drawing surfaces and media.

One section concentrates on the surface texture and colour of the materials on which drawings are made, showing the range of surfaces that have been commonly used and how their nature influences the way in which the draughtsman draws, the effect produced by him, and the viewer's response to that.

The second section concentrates on the media and implements used to make drawings, showing some of the variety of effects obtainable and how many of these differences spring from the characteristics of the materials themselves. For example, the fineness of the metal-point as a drawing implement dictates intricate movements from the draughtsman's fingers, while the coarser medium of charcoal encourages the artist to draw with bold sweeps of the arm. As a result, metal-point drawings tend to be small while works in charcoal, conceived on a broader scale, tend to be larger. The quality of the line produced with an implement such as a pen or brush, where the motion of the instrument has to be broken off to have the ink replenished, is bound to differ from the line made with, for example, graphite or chalk, each of which provide an uninterrupted supply of the medium.

Much confusion surrounds the use of terms used to describe drawing media. Particular words have been in vogue during certain periods and so have often been incorrectly used by connoisseurs, collectors and cataloguers alike, with the result that their meanings have become distorted. The use of the word 'lead', as in the expression lead pencil, is a good example of such confusions, as we shall see. The brief descriptions of the different media are given here in an attempt to clarify some of these inconsistencies, although usage continues to differ from place to place. The even briefer historical notes on the early use of

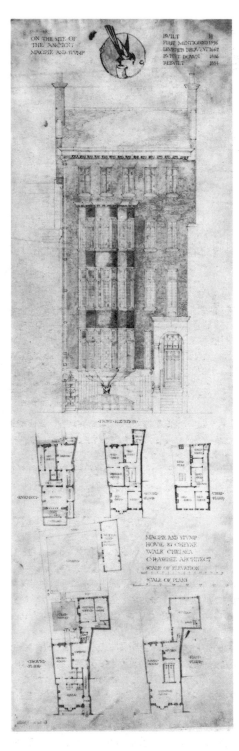

each technique aim to suggest how the appearance of new drawing materials and their subsequent popularity contributed to changes in drawing style.

A third section aims to give some insight into a number of tricks of the draughtsman's studio and some of the short cuts that can be taken in the making of a drawing.

DRAWING SURFACES

Virtually any surface, be it curved, rough or flat, or whether fixed or portable, can be drawn on. Here, examples are limited to drawings on parchment (including vellum) and paper, the materials most commonly used by artists in the West since the Middle Ages.

Until paper became a cheap commodity much drawing was done with a stylus on tablets consisting of small wooden panels surfaced with tinted wax or prepared with some kind of white ground. Such a surface could be cleaned off and renewed, allowing the same tablet to be used again and again.

Parchment and vellum

During the Middle Ages parchment and its finer form, vellum, were the principal supports that would have been used for a drawing which was to be preserved. Both parchment and vellum are made from the skin of animals, usually sheep, goats or calves, vellum being made from specially selected young skins. The surface of both parchment and vellum is prepared for drawing by being rubbed with pumice, ground bone or chalk. These smooth the skin and leave behind a hardened surface, of compacted dust. Some preparations can also be cleaned off after use and replaced, allowing the same piece of parchment to be re-used. During the Renaissance ink was often used on vellum, the effect being similar to that of an engraving (see fig. 1). The material is rarely used today by artists, except as a deliberate anachronism, as in figure 2, though both vellum and parchment are used by calligraphers.

Paper

Paper was in use in China by the second century AD, but it was not manufactured in Europe until the twelfth century. Though there are records of paper in Tuscan studios around 1300, it did not become plentiful until the fifteenth century. The texture, finish and absorbency of a sheet of paper have a considerable influence on the character of the mark made on it, so how paper is made and finished is important in understanding how artists used paper in drawings.

Paper is composed of matted fibres, originally from rags but after the nineteenth century from wood-pulp as well. It is made in a mould which looks much like a tray with a fine wire grid as its base. To make a sheet of paper the mould is dipped into liquid pulp so that the wire grid is covered with the pulp: the thickness of paper required dictates the correct amount. The wire grid is made in one of two patterns and depending on which is used, the paper is described as either 'laid' or 'wove'. For laid paper the wire network of the mould consists of parallel rows of thin wires lying close together, crossed at intervals of

3. Thomas Gainsborough (1727-1788);
British
Studies of goats, late 1780s
Black chalk heightened with white, on buff
laid paper. 17.5 x 21 cm. (detail)
The very rough paper appears to have been
scarcely pressed at all. Note how its texture
and colour play almost as important a part in
the effectiveness of the image as the chalk
marks themselves.

Gainsborough made animal studies from
life all through his career, some with no
grander composition in mind and others for
inclusion in specific paintings. This drawing is
probably related to a painting of the Prodigal
Son.
Bibl: J. Hayes, *The Drawings of Thomas
Gainsborough*, 1970, no. 227. *See* Plate IV.

2. Charles Robert Ashbee (1863-1942);
British
Elevation of Magpie and Stump House,
37 Cheyne Walk, London, 1894
Pen and ink and water-colour on vellum
82.5 x 26.9 cm.
Ashbee, founder of the Guild of Handicraft,
built the Magpie and Stump for himself; the
anachronistic use of vellum is presumably
intended to recall Renaissance drawing and to
give the drawing additional prestige.

one to one and a half inches by thicker wires. For wove paper, as the name
suggests, the mould consists of a mesh woven much like a piece of fabric. In
both types of paper the pulp is slightly thinner where it rests on the wires. This
creates different surface textures which appear either as a pattern of pale lines
or as an irregular mottling, when the paper is held up to the light (see figs 3
& 4).

Once the mould is covered with pulp, it is shaken to make sure that the pulp
is evenly distributed and that the fibres are well enmeshed. After much of the
liquid has drained away, the mould is pressed onto a piece of felt. The pulp
forming the sheet of paper sticks to this, making removal from the mould
possible. To extract the liquid further, a number of such sheets, either with or
without the felts in place, are stacked together, the weight increasing the
pressure and so driving out the remaining liquid. The individual sheets are then
hung up to dry.

To obtain the required smoothness of surface texture the sheets are
individually pressed, the pressure exerted being dictated by the desired finish.
Traditionally there are three grades of finish: hot pressed, not (meaning not hot
pressed) and rough. But within these grades a wide variety of effects can be
obtained.

Hot pressed paper is smooth. This surface is achieved by subjecting the dry
sheets, each one placed between metal plates, to mechanical pressure. Not
paper is also pressed in a mechanical press but without interleaving of any kind.

4. Specimens of Drawing Paper
An advertisement from Ackermann's
Repository, vol.III, 1810.
Grey and cream toned, and two types of
white wove papers
Artists were attracted to wove paper towards
the end of the eighteenth century on account
of its irregular surface which, if adequately
pressed, proved less obtrusive than that of laid
paper, with its furrows.

5. Conroy Maddox (born 1912); British
Personnage in a landscape, 1939
Signed and dated *Conroy Maddox 1939*
Collage and *ecrémage* (oil and water-colour
skimmed across the surface) on grounded
wove paper. 22.7 x 28.8 cm.
To create the appearance of landscape in this
picture, the artist has manipulated the chance
effects produced when oil and water-colour
are skimmed across a surface. The paper was
first prepared with a hard, smooth surface in
order to allow the oil and water to respond to
one another without interference from the
texture of the paper. Such chance effects have
been used as compositional aids by generations of artists but were particularly
attractive to artists, like Maddox, who were
adherents of Surrealism. The relationship
between chance and the artist's choice is
further explored in this picture by the use of
collaged images cut from magazines to people
the landscape.

The surface of a sheet of not paper bears, therefore, an imprint of the sheets above and below it. Rough paper is not pressed at all, the stack of sheets and felt being left to dry out under their own weight. Its surface has a felt like roughness. The Gainsborough drawing in figure 3 gains much of its vigour from the uneven surface of the paper under the chalk lines.

Usually paper is sized, in order to make it harder and the surface less absorbent. Sizing is normally undertaken before the final pressing takes place, by dipping the sheet into a vat containing a suitable glutinous substance.

The earliest ungrounded papers that have survived are thick and soft. The fibres of early European papers were very long, and good quality size, which would not yellow, was not available until about 1400.

(i) (?) Ramsey Abbey, c. 1160-1170
Bede, Commentary on the Apocalypse
St John, vested as a bishop, with a monk,
the scribe, kneeling at his feet
Pen and ink over traces of metal-point, with
some shading by brush, on vellum
27 x 17.8 cm.
This drawing is in the common technique of
pen drawing over a first outline in metal-
point. In style, it shows a hardening of
outline and a solidification of form, typical
of Romanesque art, as compared to the
earlier English drawings of the Anglo-Saxon
period. The use of outline drawing for book
illustration is relatively rare outside England
in the 12th century.
C.M. Kauffmann, *Romanesque Manuscripts
1066-1190*, 1975, no. 86.

When paper first came into use in artists' studios, it was often grounded, or rubbed with pumice as if it was parchment, so as to make it receptive to metal-point (see fig. 6). Coloured grounds quickly became fashionable. In his *Treatise on Painting*, in the chapter on 'How to draw on tinted paper' Cennino Cennini wrote: 'The tints may be either red, purple, green, azure grey, flesh-colour, or any colour you please ... It is true that green tints are the most beautiful and most frequently used ...'[3] These colours were not used solely for their inherent charm but also because they contributed to the impression of solidity of the drawn forms and enabled shadows and highlights to be executed more convincingly, as in plate II.

Integrally coloured papers, that is papers where the colour is in the body of the paper rather than just applied to the surface, first appeared towards the end of the fifteenth century. Blue paper, emanating from Venice, was the first colour to come on to the market (see plate III) and remained one of the most popular but it was quickly followed by all shades of grey and fawn (see plate IV). By the sixteenth century a range of coloured papers was the normal stock of any artist's studio.

Until the middle of the eighteenth century all European-made paper was of the kind known as 'laid'. 'Wove' paper was introduced into the West in about 1750 but it was not much used for drawing until the last two decades of the century. Until the end of the eighteenth century all paper was also made by hand and the dimensions of any sheet were limited to the size of mould that could be handled by the craftsman. When larger areas were required, as in the case of cartoons, several sheets would be pasted together. About 1799 the first machine for making continuous paper was invented. The paper was formed on an enormous wire mesh on which the width of the final sheet was limited only by that of the machine. In 1825 laid paper was first manufactured by machine and it became possible to produce paper with a great variety of novel grains, by varying the grids and the designs on the metal plates used to press paper. In the nineteenth century Japanese paper became popular, firstly for prints and later for drawings, mainly because of its fine quality and the unusual surface finishes that were available, but also because of the general interest in the Orient at that time. The fashion resulted in the production of many imitation Japanese papers like that used by Klimt in plate VI.

Cotton and linen fibre from rags was the principal ingredient in all paper until the 1840s when wood pulp was introduced. Paper made from wood pulp has a tendency to rot and to turn brown when exposed to light. Today this deterioration can, to a large extent, be counteracted by the use of chemicals, but the best quality papers are still manufactured from rags.

IMPLEMENTS AND MEDIA

Stylus

A stylus was the implement used to write on wax tablets in Classical times: it is a pointed metal rod, similar to a metal-point, but it is intended only to leave an impression on the surface rather than a mark in colour. Since then it has served many purposes. Those most relevant to us here are its use as a means of

6. Anonymous (mid-sixteenth century);
Italian
An angel holding a wreath (or crown of
thorns) in the right hand and a staff
in the left
The top of the sheet cut and inscribed with
an illegible word in ink by a later hand
Metal-point on pink prepared laid paper
16.5 x 10.1 cm.
During the Middle Ages metal-point was used
primarily for drawing outlines or as a preliminary for pen work. During the Renaissance it
was developed into an independent technique
in which works with intricate shading were
executed entirely in it. The grey colour and the
outlines of the line in this drawing suggests
that it was probably done with a lead point.
Bibl: Ward-Jackson I 516.

transferring the main lines of a composition from one sheet to another or from a cartoon to the plaster for a fresco. Before the invention of the erasable pencil, it was used to put in the guide lines of a composition, particularly perspective lines and other measurements, as can be seen in Valeriani's stage set in figure 25.

Metal-point

A metal-point is a thin rod of metal used as a drawing implement. A variety of metals can be used but lead, silver, copper and gold are the most common: see figures 6 and 7.

Lead point, often an alloy of tin and lead, is the only metal-point which leaves a mark on a smooth unprepared paper, though the mark is faint and easily erased. Lead point, known to the Romans, was widely used by apprentices and for under-drawing, from the Middle Ages until it was supplanted by graphite. Figure 6 is a sixteenth-century example of lead-point drawing.

Other metal-points require an abrasive surface if they are to leave a mark. With all metals the mark appears greyish black at first but varies from yellow to black as oxidisation takes place. It is hard to tell which metal has been used without chemical tests and so we have used the generic term metal-point throughout.

Before paper was available metal-points were used on vellum prepared in the usual way by being rubbed with pumice or chalk. Once paper came in to general use it was prepared in a similar way although the ground was often brushed on wet in several layers and could include powdered pigments.

During the Middle Ages metal-point was used primarily as a preliminary for work in pen, or for drawing outlines (see fig. i). During the Renaissance it was developed as an independent technique in which works with intricate shading were executed entirely in the medium. Because of the expense involved in the preparation of the ground and the valuable metals used to make the marks, metal-point drawings have always been highly prized. This preciosity probably contributed to its renewed popularity in the nineteenth century. Some of the compositions produced at that date were very curious as, for example, that of figure 7, where the large scale is out of character with the fineness of the medium.

Implements used with ink

Both pens and brushes have been used to draw with ink since Antiquity. Before the invention of metal nibs there were two kinds of pen; those cut from wood such as reed or bamboo, known as reed pens, and those made by shaving down long feathers, known as quills. Before the nineteenth century the majority of pen drawings were drawn with quills, made from goose, crow or swan feathers, which, as they could be pared to flexible points varying in shape from broad to finely tapered, provided the artist with a very versatile instrument. But reed pens, which quills superseded as writing instruments, were sometimes used when the broad, accented, vigorous effects which are characteristic of their stroke were called for. Reed pens are prepared in a similar way to quills, the

7. Charles Prosper Sainton (1861-1914); British
The Stars
Signed, and dated 92
Metal-point. 54.5 x 42 cm.
There was a revival of interest in metal-point in the nineteenth century. Sainton uses the point to produce subtle shading reminiscent of photography, which may indeed have been employed to catch the poses of the figures for this composition. Other contemporary artists also used metal-point for its linear qualities almost as a graphic equivalent of etching. It is probable that this drawing was intended for a book illustration.

8. Giacomo Cortese (Jacques Courtois)
known as il Borgognone (1621-1676); Italian
A cavalry skirmish
Inscribed in a later hand *Bourguignon*
Reed pen and ink over red chalk,
with touches of grey wash, on laid paper.
19 x 30.8 cm.

9. Giulio Cesare Procaccini (1574-1625);
Italian
Sheet of studies including a Virgin and
Child, the heads of two angels, a youth and
a draped female. On the verso there are
more studies. The sheet is stamped and
inscribed with the collector's marks of
Earl Spencer (Lugt 1530) and W. Esdaille
(Lugt 2617)
Brush with coloured ink washes on laid
paper. 22.2 x 28.6 cm. (detail)
Lines made with a brush tend to be softer
than pen marks, and often taper to a point
where the brush has been lifted off the
paper.
Bibl: Ward-Jackson I 260. *See* Plate V.

10. Hans Baldung (called Grien)
(c. 1480-1545); German
Design for a stained glass window, probably commissioned about 1508 by Veronica of Andlau on her becoming Abbess of the Convent of Hohenberg (Odilienberg), Alsace. Inscribed *Item vi nunnen vier nach einander und zwo dahinden als gross sie syn mogen hinderen pfeyler lond euch nit irren oder den rottelstrich.* (Item, six nuns four one behind the other, and two in the background, of the required size. By the pillars at the back do not be led into error, nor by the red chalk). Pen and black and brown inks and red chalk on laid paper.
42.9 x 31.5 cm.
Presumably both iron-gall and carbon inks were used in this drawing. It is an interesting example of the design process in sixteenth-century stained-glass manufacture. The architectural elements and the armorial shields appear to be drawn in a hand different from that which drew the figures, and it is likely that they are by a draughtsman from the glass workshop which had been commissioned to make the panel. The draughtsman thus provided the structural framework within which Baldung was to work in supplying the figures of the six nuns, and it is probable that the written instructions are from him to Baldung also.
Bibl: C. Koch, *Die Zeichnungen Hans Baldung Griens*, 1941, no. 71. *See* Plate X.

sides of the reed's stem being cut away to create nibs of the desired shape, though their fibrous structure and overall thickness make them better adapted to retaining broad blunt tips than delicate points. Reed pens tend to shed ink more quickly than quills and therefore produce short, interrupted lines rather than the meandering arabesques of which the quill is capable. Unless the lines show these marked characteristics, it can, however, be difficult to identify whether a reed or quill has been used, especially if the reed has been pared to the narrowest point it will hold or if the quill has been cut bluntly. The drawing by Cortese (fig. 8) was executed with a reed pen, whereas that in figure 10, for example, was probably drawn with a quill. Metal nibs are first recorded in the sixteenth century but they were not widely used as drawing implements until the nineteenth century.

Iron-gall ink

It is difficult to distinguish the ingredients of the medium used in what is loosely described as an 'ink' drawing. Most Renaissance drawings were executed in traditional writing ink, known as iron-gall ink, made, as the name suggests, from a suspension of iron salts in gallic acid obtained from the nutgall, a growth on certain oak trees caused by disease. Although almost black when applied iron-gall ink turns brown with time, as the acid eats into the paper.

Carbon ink

Carbon ink is made from soot of one form or another, or some other easily available carbon dissolved in water, often with a binder such as gum arabic added. This kind of ink does not turn brown or fade. (Indian ink is a waterproof form of carbon ink in which some kind of resin has been dissolved. This gives the ink a sheen.) Although known for thousands of years in the East, detailed recipes for the manufacture of carbon ink did not appear in Europe until the sixteenth century. At this time it was used far more commonly in Germany than in Italy. The drawing by Hans Baldung (fig. 10). which uses both carbon and iron-gall ink, is an early example of its use: the difference in colour can be seen in plate X.

Bistre

Bistre ink or wash is made from wood soot dissolved in water. Its colour varies from brownish yellow to a deep blackish brown depending on the type of wood burned and the concentration of soot in the ink. It is difficult to distinguish bistre from other brownish inks but one of its characteristics is the uneven granulated surface produced by undissolved particles, which can be seen on the Tiepolo drawing in figure 11. Bistre was used in the Middle Ages but the term did not become current until the sixteenth century and was not widely used until the eighteenth century.

11. Giovanni Battista Tiepolo (1696-1770);
Italian
The Banquet of Anthony and Cleopatra.
A study for an oil sketch in the National
Gallery, London, (no. 6409), itself for a
painting in the Yousoupoff Palace,
Leningrad.
Pen and bistre wash over black chalk on laid
paper. 23.5 x 33.5 cm.
The undissolved brown particles of bistre
are clearly visible.
Bibl. George Knox, *Catalogue of Tiepolo
Drawings in the Victoria and Albert Museum*,
no. 85.

Sepia

Much confusion surrounds the term sepia which is often used to describe
various tones of brownish wash. True sepia is obtained from the inky secretion
of the cuttle-fish, which produces an ink that gives a smooth transparent effect.
Latin sources refer to its occasional use in writing but it does not appear as a
drawing medium until the eighteenth century. It became fashionable among
both professional and amateur artists in the nineteenth century: our example is
by Henry Pierce Bone (fig. 12).

I Bernardo Parentino. *See* fig. 1.

Antonio Poll

650

II. Fra Bartolommeo (Baccio della Porta) (1472-1517); Italian
A seated man, holding a tablet on his knee
Inscribed in ink *Del frate*, with the collector's mark of Sir Joshua Reynolds (Lugt 2364)
Black chalk on pink tinted paper. 20.6 x 13 cm.
The rust-coloured spots on this drawing are due to impurities in the paper.
Bibl: Ward-Jackson I 40.

III. Jacopo Tintoretto (1518-1594); Italian
A kneeling monk

12. Henry Pierce Bone (1779-1855); British
Cupid dipped in wine
Illustration to the sixth ode of Anacreon.
Sepia wash over pencil on wove paper
32 x 42.4 cm.
The Sketching Society met to draw in a
single evening a set subject; this subject was
given on the 14th December 1821. The rules
stated that the medium was to be sepia;
such ink drawings can be executed quickly
giving a good tonal range.

IV Thomas Gainsborough. *See* fig. 3.
V Giulio Cesare Procaccini. *See* fig. 9.

Water-colour

Water-colour is any pigment dissolved in water and bound with some kind of
gum, usually gum arabic, so it could be said that all inks are water-colour. The
term technically includes opaque forms such as body colour, but it is more
often restricted to describing transparent washes. Pure water-colour painting,
in which the drawn line plays no structural part, emerged in the eighteenth
century in England. It was particularly suitable for landscape and architectural
subjects (such as the Peter de Wint drawing in figure 13) because of the
combined effects of the solidity of the colour and the luminosity of the paper
beneath.

13. Peter de Wint (1784–1849); British
Potter Gate, Lincoln
Water-colour. 28.8 x 39.8 cm.
Pure water-colour painting, in which the drawn line is entirely eliminated, emerged in the late eighteenth century. The combined effect of luminosity (due to the white paper beneath) and solidity make it a particularly effective medium for landscape.

14. Franciabigio (Francesco di Cristofano) (?1482-1525); Italian
Head of a young man
With the collector's mark of J. Richardson Jr (Lugt 2170)
Black chalk with touches of white on laid paper. 25.1 x 20.6 cm.
Bibl: Ward-Jackson I 136.

Charcoal

Charcoal, a form of carbon, is the residue of wood burnt in a restricted supply of oxygen. Myrtle, walnut, birch and willow twigs are among the woods which have been used to make charcoal drawing sticks. Charcoal was used as a drawing medium for sketching in free-hand large-scale mural compositions by the Greeks and Romans and during the Middle Ages and the Renaissance. Nevertheless there is no evidence that it was much used for drawing on paper until the beginning of the sixteenth century. This may be because no such drawings were made, or because fixatives were not available and the charcoal has been rubbed away. The ease with which charcoal can be erased has made it a popular medium for both preliminary sketches and the drawing of cartoons as well as a method of laying in the main lines of a composition. As plate VII shows, it can also be used for dramatic and effective rapid sketches, here of a

15. Andrea del Sarto (1486-1530); Italian
Study for the head of Jesus
Used for the painting of the Holy Family
in the Palazzo Barberini, Rome.
Red chalk on laid paper. 14.5 x 11.7 cm.
During the last twenty years of his life, Andrea
del Sarto showed a preference for red chalk.
He was in Paris in 1518, and this may have
contributed to the enthusiasm with which the
medium was taken up in France.
Bibl: Ward-Jackson I 313.

nude figure. Charcoal can be made self-fixing if it is soaked in oil. Lines drawn
in charcoal treated in this way tend to have a yellowish 'halo' spreading out
from both sides of the stroke, as in the head by Gauguin, illustrated as
figure 77.

Chalk

The use of chalk as a drawing medium had a great influence on style. Although
chalk can be sharpened to a point it quickly wears down and cannot produce the
fine strokes of a metal-point or pen. As a result artists were encouraged to draw

in a freer manner on a broader scale. The use of chalk of all colours was stimulated by the availability of integrally coloured paper. By the middle of the sixteenth century a profusion of techniques including all kinds of colours of chalks, graphite, pen and ink and wash is often found in one drawing.

Black chalk

Natural black chalk is a mineral that makes an indelible mark. Although known to Cennino Cennini it appears to have been little used until towards the end of the fifteenth century, becoming popular during the sixteenth century. Artificial chalk made from carbon was also available in the sixteenth century. Although the former may leave scratches from gritty impurities and the latter tends to be darker and richer, in practice it is difficult to distinguish which kind of chalk has been used. The drawings in figures 3 and 14 are among the many in black chalk illustrated here.

Red chalk

Red chalk, also described as sanguine, consists of red ferrous oxide, a dry earth pigment that has been known to man for thousands of years: it was used to draw the outlines on Egyptian tomb paintings and in Roman frescoes. Nevertheless, during the Renaissance it lagged behind black chalk in popularity. It has been suggested that this is because there was no fixative available for red chalk before 1480. It may also be that, at a time when metal-point was being superseded, red chalk seemed garish in comparison to black. Leonardo was the first major artist to use red chalk. His lead was quickly followed, for example by Andrea del Sarto (fig. 15), and during the sixteenth century the medium became popular on its own and in combination with others, particularly black chalk. The Holbein school drawing in figure 23 is a splendid example. During the eighteenth century in France red chalk drawing (see, for example, the Watteau drawing in figure 71) gave rise to a fashion for a particular sort of imitative print, made in the 'crayon manner'.

Pastel

Pastels are sticks of variously coloured powdered pigments mixed with white. The range of colours available, and the way in which they blend together when applied have led to pastels being considered a dry form of painting. Pastel was known in the fifteenth century, but became particularly popular during the eighteenth century, its delicate colouring being in keeping with the Rococo spirit. John Russell's portrait of a young girl (fig. 16) is a typical example.

Graphite

Graphite, a crystalline form of carbon, also known as plumbago, is the material from which pencils are made. There are signs that it was first used for under-drawing in the sixteenth century, supplanting the lead point. From this association the misleading term 'lead pencil' seems to have arisen, though the word plumbago also means lead.

17. Thomas Forster (worked c. 1690-1713);
British
Portrait of an unknown man
Signed and dated *T. Forster delin 1702*
Graphite ('plumbago') on vellum
10 x 8.5 cm.
The use of graphite, even in its pure soft form,
enabled miniaturists to achieve a richness and
delicacy of treatment impossible in any other
graphic medium. Forster here combines
delicate line-work with block tone reminiscent
of contemporary mezzotints. Early graphite
miniatures are usually described as being
executed in plumbago.

In Britain graphite began to be mined on a large scale in Cumberland in 1664. In 1795 Nicolas-Jacques Conté patented a process for making pencils of varying degrees of hardness, to order, by mixing graphite with clay. This reliability, combined with versatility, greatly increased the pencil's popularity especially in England, as a sketching medium (see fig. 18). Much confusion surrounds the terms graphite, plumbago and pencil. Early examples of graphite, such as the portrait by Thomas Forster in figure 17, are often referred to as plumbago, while graphite cased in wood is usually called pencil. In the past the term pencil was used to describe a pointed brush, while what we now call Conté crayons are not pencils but greasy chalks, often used uncased.

DRAWING CONVENTIONS AND DRAWING AIDS

16. John Russell, RA (1745-1806); British
Study for a portrait of an unknown girl
Pastel on blue-grey laid paper. 29.5 x 26 cm.
Russell modelled his technique on the work of
the famous Venetian pastellist Rosalba
Carriera (1675-1757). He himself was the
author of *The Elements of Painting with Crayons*,
(1772).

The most important problem an artist who wishes to represent three dimensions in two has to solve is how to recreate the effect of binocular vision, and various methods of perspective have been developed to deal with this. Drawing manuals expounded at length on the subject of perspective systems, and a number of mechanical aids for drawing in perspective, such as the camera lucida, shown in use in figure 24, have also been devised.

Another problem is that most drawings are produced as preliminary works. For this reason they often need to be transferred on to another surface, either so

18. Thomas Girtin (1775-1802); British
King John's Palace, Eltham
Signed *T. Girtin* and inscribed with title;
inscribed similarly on the back
Graphite ('pencil') on cream wove paper
31.2 x 27.4 cm.
The drawing dates from the period of Girtin's
involvement in the so-called 'Monro School',
an association of young artists who met at the
house of Dr Thomas Monro in Adelphi Terrace
in London in order to study landscape and
architectural drawings in his collection.
Something like a 'house style' seems to have
been worked out amongst the artists concerned,
and it is usually impossible to be at all precise
in attribution. One can however often recognise
Girtin's hand, here attested by his signature,
but almost always distinctive in its nervous
and strikingly vivid use of the graphite medium.
He was the most brilliant practitioner of a way
of drawing that was capable of describing
variations in surface texture or the intricate
details of an architectural façade with a fullness
and rapid economy difficult in any other
medium.

Quite largely on Girtin's example the style
became dominant as a sketch medium in the
English School and often, in the work of
Cotman or Varley for example, it provided the
firm structural underpinning of finished water-
colours.

Bibl: T. Girtin & D. Loshak, *The Art of Thomas
Girtin*, 1954, no. 137.

that the artist can continue to work out his ideas or to provide a design for work
in another medium. Also, the artist may need to correct his drawing, and this
chapter ends with an example of such corrections. Correction must be
distinguished from conservation, which is often necessary to preserve works on
paper, but which can pose problems of appreciation, as figure 33
demonstrates.

Perspective

Perspective is the art of representing with a flat (or at least shallower) surface
than that represented, the effect of solidity and relative distance and size. Two
main groups of phenomena are exploited in the creation of such impressions,
and so there are are two distinct types of perspective: linear and aerial. Linear

VI. Gustav Klimt (1862-1918); Austrian
Study of two reclining female nudes
Stamped in ink *Gustav Klimt Nachlass* (Lugt 1575)
Blue chalk on cream Japanese paper. 20 x 56 cm.
The popularity of oriental papers for printmaking in the West in the nineteenth century spread to
drawing papers early during this century, since when many imitations have been manufactured.
Here the spare lines of the drawing are set off by the silky finish of the paper.

VII. Henri Gaudier-Brzeska (1891-1915);
French, worked in Britain
Study of a standing female nude
Charcoal on wove paper. 50 x 20 cm.
The broadly applied charcoal effectively
expresses the blocky highly-lit forms.
Bibl: H. Brodzky, *Gaudier-Brezska Drawings*,
1946, no. 63.

19. John Prizeman (born 1930); British
Design for a kitchen for Michael Crawford,
to be made by Hygena Kitchens, 1975
Inscribed with title
Pen and ink and 'Letratone' on tracing
paper. 37 x 26 cm.
This is an 'artist's impression' of a finished
kitchen. 'Letratone', a transferable sheet
printed with dotted toning which can be laid
onto the drawing, replaces hatching or washes.
Similar semi-mechanical toning has been used
by illustrators since the 1920s. The pattern
of the floor tiles shows the use of linear
perspective.

perspective is a quasi-mathematical system based on the theory that parallel
lines, as they recede, give the illusion of converging and that all those lines going
in any one direction meet at a single point on the horizon. Figure 20 shows a
linear perspective system, probably drawn for a manual. The drawings by
Canaletto (fig. 59, where the vanishing point can be seen in the preliminary
drawing) and Guardi (fig. 60) show linear perspective in use. Aerial perspective

20. Anonymous; Italian
A lesson in perspective showing a method
of drawing towers from a point above them.
c. 1780
Inscribed *Leze VIII* and *V. Fig 8*
Pen and ink and water-colour on laid paper
54.5 x 42.5 cm.
This eighteenth century diagram is typical of
the illustrations for the manuals on perspective. It is intended to explain aspects of linear
perspective but in fact the effect of depth in the
scene with the towers is increased by the use of
aerial perspective, the ground and sky being
painted in graduated bands of colour.

21. Tobias Verhaeght (1561-1631); Flemish
A mountainous landscape with a river flowing through; a castle on a crag to the right and a town with a bridge in the near middle-distance.
Pen and ink and wash with additional blue-grey wash on laid paper
24.7 x 38.5 cm.

One of the standard phenomena of perspective is that objects in the distance appear smaller than objects of a similar size which are closer to the viewpoint. In this drawing the artist has achieved a sense of depth by making the pen stroke the measure. By reducing the size of the strokes towards the horizon he has created his own graphic system of aerial perspective, in place of the traditional system of graded tone and colour.

depends for its effect on a scaled variation of colour which represents the effect of atmosphere on the perception of colour, tone and form at different distances. The effect of depth in the inset scene of figure 20 is enhanced by aerial perspective, and a form of aerial perspective is used by Tobias Verhaeght for the landscape in figure 21. The 'discovery' of perspective dates from the Renaissance, a time when theoretical knowledge was increasingly replacing empiricism. Brunelleschi is claimed as the first person to have made a mathematical study of the laws underlying linear perspective but Alberti, in *De Pittura*, written in 1436, was the first to set them out in writing for the use of painters. Within a hundred years such rules had become required learning for every apprenticed artist, and manuals expounding them proliferated.

Among the mechanical aids invented to assist in depicting perspective was the camera lucida. Patented by William Hyde Wallaston, it was developed from the camera obscura. The latter, used since the Middle Ages, consisted originally of a dark room in which an image of the world outside was allowed to enter through a tiny hole in one wall and fall upon a surface, so that it could be copied or traced. A portable version consisting of a box with a lens, mirror (the

22. Albrecht Dürer (1471-1528); German
A draughtsman drawing a portrait
Page from *Underweysung der Messung*, first
published with German text in Nuremberg,
1525, from either the Paris or Arnheim
editions with Latin texts, both published
1532
Woodcut. 13 x 14.8 cm.
This illustration shows the use of a drawing
aid which facilitates the representation of
three dimensions on a flat surface. The
artist sketches the main lines of the sitter
onto a frosted glass panel placed between
them. To keep the same viewpoint while
making the sketch the artist squints through
a peephole. The following illustration,
no. 23, was drawn using a device of this
kind.

23. School of Hans Holbein (?)
(1497/8-1543); British
Portrait of an unknown gentleman
From the collection of Padre Resta, and
stamped with a late 17th or early 18th
century collector's mark (Lugt 2908)
Coloured chalks reinforced with metal-point
on pink-toned laid paper. 35 x 26.6 cm.
The startlingly photographic quality of
Holbein's portrait drawings in the Royal
Collection at Windsor Castle, which were
prepared as accurate studies for paintings,
may be partly the result of the use of a
tracing apparatus such as that shown in
figure 22. Certainly their flattened, simplified images and reinforced outlines are
suggestive of the two-dimensional effect of
an object viewed by a single eye. This
drawing, with its cut corners, may have
been part of the Windsor group and it
shares their qualities, but its handling,
notably in the drapery, is uneven, and it was
not included by Paul Ganz in his catalogue
raisonné of Holbein drawings. The pink
ground, also characteristic of Holbein's
Windsor drawings, not only helped in the
rendering of flesh tones but also allowed the
use of metal-point.
Bibl: K.T. Parker, *The Drawings of Hans
Holbein in the collection of His Majesty the
King*, 1945, p. 30f.

image in a camera obscura is normally inverted) and ground-glass screen from
which the image could be drawn, was invented in the seventeenth century. The
main difference between the camera obscura and the camera lucida is that the
latter can be used in daylight. It consists of a glass prism which can be revolved
on the end of an adjustable arm. The user looks into the prism with one eye,
while looking past it on to his paper, where there hovers a reduced, transparent
image of the scene at which the other face of the prism is pointed. Thus the
instrument provides a means of representing a scene in perspective without
involving the conscious application of the rules of linear perspective.

24. Henry Moses (c.1782-1870); British
A woman sketching a child with the aid
of a camera lucida
From a series of 15 drawings of female
costume dated 1818 to 1836
Pencil and red chalk on wove paper
7.5 x 10.8 cm.

25. Guiseppe Valeriani (1708-1762); Italian,
worked in Russia
A hall in a palace
Design for a stage setting, possibly for the
opera *Scipio* by Francesco Araja, produced
at the court theatre, St Petersburg,
29 August 1745
With the collector's mark of Edmond Fatio
Pen and ink and brown wash and pencil on
laid paper; indented with a stylus and
blackened on the back. 28.1 x 24.5 cm.
The artist has taken care to transfer the
architectural perspective. The figures could
be added freehand.

Transfer methods

A number of different ways of transferring drawings from one surface to
another have been developed. The back of the drawing can be rubbed with
chalk, charcoal or graphite, and the lines of the drawing impressed with a
stylus, so that the back of the sheet acts as a kind of carbon paper.

Another method, known as squaring, or squaring-up, is to rule on the design
and the surface on to which it is to be transferred a grid of horizontal and
vertical lines, so that it is easy to identify where each section of the design
should be copied. This method is equally effective for reducing or enlarging a
design, simply by varying the ratio between the two sets of squares, and it is
often used to produce full-size cartoons, like figure 86. Figures 26 and 32 show
drawings that have been squared up for enlargement. Another method of
transferring designs to a different scale is to use a pantograph, a machine which
uses a set of adjustable levers between two arms: one arm traces the outlines of
the original design, and a drawing instrument attached to the other draws out
the design to scale. One manual, Albrecht Dürer's *Underweysung der Messung*
(Nuremberg, 1525), shows an artist drawing on squared paper with a grid
placed between his subject and himself. This not only allowed the actual
drawing to be scaled up or down as needed but also helped in the representation
of foreshortening, by acting as a guide to the relative proportions of his
subject.

Another method of transfer is known as pouncing. This involves pricking the
contours of the design with a needle or pin, and rubbing coloured powder
through the holes onto a second sheet of paper: the resulting pattern of coloured

26. Robert Polhill Bevan (1865-1925);
British
The feathered hat
Study for a portrait of the artist's wife.
c. 1915
Stamped in ink with the artist's monogram
Black chalk, squared and numbered for
transfer on wove paper
Size of sheet 36 x 40.5 cm.
Bibl: R.A. Bevan, *Robert Bevan*, 1965,
fig. 56.

dots follows the original design. The drawings by De Morgan (fig. 28) and D'Oggiono (fig. 27) have been pricked for transfer.

Counter-proofing is a transfer method which results in a reversed image and therefore has rather specialized uses. To take a counterproof a thin sheet of moistened paper is pressed onto a drawing, either in a printing press or by burnishing, so that some of the pigment of the original comes off onto the sheet. Drawings that are intended to be turned into prints are often counterproofed so that the printmaker does not have to work with a mirror or reverse the image in his head in order to make the print in the same sense as the drawing. The technique can also be used to produce the second half of a symmetrical design or to get the effect of a repeat pattern in, for example, designs for ceramic wares

27. Marco D'Oggiono (died after 1524);
Italian
Head of the Virgin
Inscribed in ink in a later hand *Raphaelo*
Urbino. L'on dit que c'est le Portrait de sa
Maitresse.
With the collector's mark of C. Josi
(Lugt 573)
Black chalk on laid paper; pricked for
transfer. 16.8 x 13.9 cm.
This drawing has been pricked for transfer,
perhaps to the painting by D'Oggiono of the
Virgin and Child in the National Gallery,
London (no. 1149), in which the head has
nearly the same dimensions.
Bibl: Ward-Jackson I 211.

28. William De Morgan (1839-1917); British
Design for the ruby lustre decoration on a
dish
Dated *June 79*
Water-colour over pencil on wove paper;
pricked for transfer. Diameter 36 cm.
The entire design has been pricked for
transfer to the dry biscuit body of the dish,
and bears traces of charcoal on the back. At
this date De Morgan's lustre ware was made
in Hanley and decorated in his Chelsea
studio, in London.

or textiles (fig. 30). Some artists, for example Rowlandson (figs 31 a & b), also
used the technique in order to produce large numbers of drawings quickly.

Today the availability of good-quality transparent tracing paper, and the use
of photographic projection techniques have tended to obviate the need for most
of these methods. The designs in figures 19 and 29 show tracing paper in use for
practical reasons: a more unusual application of the material can be seen in the
Sol LeWitt drawing in plate XX.

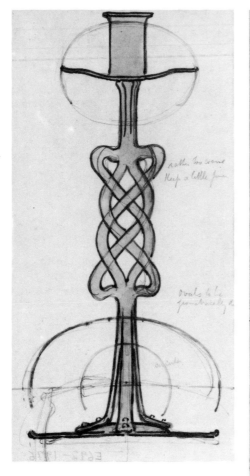

29. Nelson Ethelred Dawson (1859-1942);
British
Design for an iron candlestick
Inscribed with notes
Pencil, water-colour wash and brush and
ink on tracing paper. 34 x 18 cm.
Good quality tracing paper was introduced
towards the end of the nineteenth century
and took the place of a number of
traditional transfer methods. Here it enables
a final working drawing to be produced very
rapidly. The blue wash has been applied to
the back of the sheet to prevent the ink lines
from being obscured.

30. Joseph Neil Paton (1797-1874) or an
assistant; British
Design for a woven damask, *c.* 1850-60
Black chalk on wove paper, counterproofed
29 x 27 cm.
The original drawing occupies the top left-
hand corner of the sheet: the rest is made up
of two counterproofs. Paton was a principal
designer for a number of damask manufacturers in Dunfermline and elsewhere in
Scotland. His son, the painter Sir Joseph
Noel Paton, may have produced some of the
designs now in the collection of the Victoria
and Albert Museum.

31. Thomas Rowlandson (1756-1827);
British
Scene on a towing-path
Original drawing and counterproof
Counterproof signed *Rowlandson*
Reed pen and ink and water-colour on wove
paper. 20.5 x 28 & 18 x 27 cm.
Rowlandson repeated drawings for sale by
working up and colouring a counterproof of
an original pen drawing. In this case (which
is perhaps a view taken beside the river
Thames) the original itself has been worked
up, strengthened with pencil, and coloured.
The deception was frequently increased by
counterproofing the original pencil lines
also, thus giving the unwary the impression
of a spontaneous sketch following a rough
outline.
Bibl: J. Hayes, *Rowlandson watercolours and
drawings*, 1972, pp. 41, 42.

32. Bernardino Gatti (il Sojaro)
(1495/1500-1576); Italian
Reclining sibyl holding a book
A study for a fresco
Inscribed in an old hand *Cesare da Sesto*
Black chalk, pen and ink, heightened with
white on grey laid paper; squared in black
chalk. 19 x 33.3 cm.
This drawing is made up of several bits of
paper carefully pieced together and is
corrected with details, such as the right
hand of the putti, stuck on.
Bibl: Ward-Jackson I 147.

Corrections

There are a number of different ways of correcting a drawing. Some drawing media can be rubbed out with bread crumbs, pumice or the more modern eraser. If the paper or parchment has a ground, the ground can be cut away around the damaged area and a new ground put in. If there is no ground, the paper itself can be cut away and a fresh piece of paper to the required shape substituted (this has been done on the drawing in figure 32, for example). Sometimes the correction on a new piece of paper is simply pasted over the old sheet. Another method is to cover the area with opaque pigment. Opaque white is particularly effective on modern artwork intended for photographic reproduction, as it is not always picked up by the camera, though it may discolour with age, as can be seen in figure 92.

33. Rembrandt Harmensz van Rijn
(1606-1669); Dutch
Landscape with a man sitting on a sluice-
gate. *c.* 1652-54
With the collectors' marks of J. Richardson
Senior (Lugt 2184) and W. Esdaile (Lugt
1617)
Pen and ink on laid paper. 14.6 x 25.4 cm.
This drawing is included as a warning
against the hazards of conservation. The
first reproduction of it has been made from
a cracked glass negative taken before
conservation was undertaken early in this
century; the second shows the drawing as it
is now. While foxing and other ravages of
time have been successfully removed, so has
some of the vibrancy of the drawing. The
balance between its lights and darks has
been disturbed and some of the finer details
have disappeared altogether. The paper has
been washed and pressed leaving it arti-
ficially smooth and entirely different from
the sheet on which the artist drew. It can
also be argued that the cleaning has
obscured part of the drawing's history.
Bibl: O. Benesch, *The Drawings of
Rembrandt*, 1954-57, vol.6 no. 1299.

DRAWING AS A DISCIPLINE

At least since 1400, when Cennini was writing his treatise on painting, Western man has regarded drawing as the founding discipline of his creative activities. Vasari tells us that Baccio Bandinelli's father, a Florentine goldsmith, held drawing classes for his apprentices 'for a man was not then considered a good goldsmith unless he could draw well'.[4] In England, William Shipley held private drawing classes at the Society of Arts (later the Royal Society of Arts) founded in 1754 for the encouragement of arts, manufactures and commerce, and Thomas Sheraton wrote a drawing-book for cabinet makers and upholsterers, in which the frontispiece depicted the 'artist busy designing' surrounded by allegorical figures of Geometry, Perspective, the Genius of Drawing and Architecture, and 'on the back ground is the Temple of Fame, to which a knowledge of these arts directly leads'. Marc Brunel, himself a distinguished engineer, encouraged his more famous son, Isambard, to sketch his surroundings, considering this habit to be as important to the engineer as a knowledge of the alphabet. When Mechanics Institutes were set up around England following the foundation of the London Mechanics Institution in 1823, architectural, mechanical and perspective drawing were among the subjects taught. In France, Ingres claimed 'Drawing is three quarters of painting...' 'If I were to hang out my sign I should write on it *Ecole de Dessin*, and I know that I should educate painters.'[5] The drawings in this chapter have been selected to illustrate the part drawing has played in the development of artists and designers of various leanings since the Renaissance: they begin with scenes of artists drawing, and show that little has changed between Mattia Preti's group of seventeenth-century figures (plate VIII) and Franklin White's sketching group of the 1930s (fig. 35).

During the fourteenth century, the training of artists was centred on the master's workshop. Cennini advised the aspiring painter that 'In the first place you must study drawing for at least one year; then you must remain with a master at the workshop for the space of six years at least, that you may learn all the parts and members of the art, – to grind colours, to boil down glues, to grind plaster, to acquire the practise of laying grounds on pictures, to work in relief, and to scrape (or smooth) the surface, and to gild; afterwards to practise colouring, to adorn with mordants, paint cloths of gold and paint on walls, for six more years, – drawing without intermission on holidays and work-days.'[6] As the status of the artist grew and the power over them of the guilds relaxed, this

34. Guercino (Giovanni Francesco Barbieri)
(1591-1666); Italian
Portrait of an artist
Pen and ink. 22.2 x 18 cm.
The artist is drawing a landscape with a quill
pen. The picture on the easel is of a female
nude.
Bibl: Ward-Jackson II 719.

practical work was supplemented by gatherings, informal at first, where drawings and antique sculpture were provided as patterns to copy and theoretical matters were discussed. From such meetings were to evolve the private and later the public academies with their rigid curricula. Michelangelo attended Bertoldo's Sculpture School in the garden of Lorenzo the Magnificent in Florence in around 1490 where, according to Vasari, drawings made by artists such as Donatello, Brunelleschi, Masaccio, Uccello, Fra Angelico and Filippo Lippi were preserved along with the antique works which inspired them, to be used as models by newcomers to the school.[7] In 1563 Cosimo de Medici founded the more formal Accademia del Disegno, and this initiative was

VIII. Mattia Preti (il Cavalier Calabrese) (1613-1699); Italian
A group of artists drawing
Inscribed on the old mount *Calabrese*
Red chalk. 24.8 x 36.5 cm.
This drawing was originally catalogued as anonymous, but a similar drawing in Düsseldorf, showing the Academy of the Carracci, by Pietro Paolo Bonzi, known as il Gobbo dei Carracci (the hunchback), has led to the suggestion that this drawing may be by him also.
Bibl: Ward-Jackson II 789.

IX. Thomas Rowlandson (1756-1827); British
Dr Syntax sketching a waterfall
Pen and ink, and water-colour. 13 x 22 cm.
Rowlandson's satirical invention, Dr Syntax, an amateur artist and connoisseur, was the subject of his *The Tour of Dr Syntax, in Search of the Picturesque*, published with a text by William Combe in Ackermann's *Poetical Magazine* from 1809 and as a single volume in 1812. This is an unpublished drawing from the series, and shows Syntax, himself an example of the picturesque, sketching a waterfall.

followed by the setting up of similar institutions in the major artistic centres in Italy from the end of the century. In 1648 the Academie Royale de Peinture et de Sculpture was founded in Paris, giving rise to the opening of art schools on the same pattern in thirty-six major French cities. During the eighteenth century academies of art sprang up all over Europe, the Royal Academy in London being founded in 1768.

Whether training took place in a master's workshop, a private school or one of the public academies it followed much the same pattern. Beginning by copying from two-dimensional works such as drawings and prints by established masters, the student graduated to the more difficult task of representing three dimensions in two, first from selected static forms such as antique sculptures and plaster casts, and then from the life. Until the nineteenth century the latter was usually confined to drawing from the model, though sketching and drawing landscapes in the open air has always been a diversion of artists, art students and amateurs, as for example the redoutable Dr Syntax (plate IX). The extent of the theoretical knowledge thought to be essential to the artist has varied in keeping with the state of learning generally and according to each moment's favoured formula, but from the mid-sixteenth century anatomy, geometry and perspective became regular subjects of study. The organisation of the illustrations in this chapter follows traditional teaching practice, showing first in figures 36 to 40 drawn copies from the flat, by artists such as Goya (fig. 38) and David (fig. 39), then copies from the round in figures 41 to 47, and finally in figures 48 to 53 drawings from the life, by Constable and Léger among others.

Within this framework there have been many variations but despite changes in the theory behind it, the primacy of drawing has remained until well into this century. Cennini, whose approach to representation was basically instinctive, recommended drawing mainly as a means of acquiring manual dexterity. This has, of course, remained an important attribute of the artist, but during the Renaissance drawing was also seen as a tool with which to gather information and to sort it into systems. Having used drawing in this way himself, Leonardo recommended that the student painter need not go back to first principles but that he should benefit from the research of others. 'The young man should first learn perspective, then the proportions of all objects. Next, copy work after the hand of a good master, to gain the habit of drawing parts of the body well; and then to work from nature, to confirm the lessons learned.'[8] Rembrandt encouraged his students to copy both his own drawings and the works of others, and he made many copies himself. According to the inventory of his possessions made at the time of his bankruptcy in 1656 he possessed prints after Vanni, Baroccio, Raphael, Antonio Tempesta, the Carracci, Guido Reni, Mantegna and Michelangelo.

During the sixteenth and seventeenth centuries many manuals setting out everything the artist needed to know, including information on anatomy, proportion, perspective and geometry were published: a treatise such as Lomazzo's *A tracte containing the artes of curious paintinge, carvinge and buildinge*, first published in Italian in 1584 and first published in England in 1598, was in use widely until the nineteenth century. The book assumed that the arts are

X Hans Baldung. *See* fig. 10. Presumably both iron-gall and carbon inks have been used here. Red chalk lines are often used to show cutting lines but here they are used to indicate the general layout.

35. Franklin White (1892-1975); British
The summer class at Shoreham, c. 1931
Signed in pencil *Franklin White*
Red chalk and pen and ink. 27.5 x 37.5 cm.

36. *After* Andrea Mantegna (1431-1506);
Envy inciting the Marine Gods to fight
Pen and ink, 28.3 x 42 cm.; engraving cut to
28 x 82.7 cm.
Ward-Jackson commented on this drawing
'An unusually accurate and sensitively
drawn copy, of exactly the same size as
the original, probably contemporary. The
copyist follows the original line by line,
except in the hatching, where his lines are
finer and closer together.' This copy may
have been made to record the original as
much as a drawing exercise.
Bibl: Ward-Jackson I 13.

subject to rules, and that the appropriate solution could be found for all of the
problems the artist might encounter. Lomazzo's work, and his approach, were
copied for many other drawing manuals. Other manuals were published
promulgating shortcuts and mechanical solutions to problems: often these
were aimed at those not necessarily with artistic talent but for whom drawing
was a necessary skill, such as draughtsmen and engineers, or the ever-growing
number of amateurs.

The insistence on rules was taken to an extreme by the academies where the
curriculum was based on the belief that the arts could be taught and learnt
through set precepts. On the foundation of the French Academy, only drawing,
theoretical lectures and analyses of the students' work were undertaken on the
premises. In figure-work not only were proportions required to conform to a
prescribed ideal but even formulae for facial expressions conveying different
emotions were produced: in 1702 Charles Le Brun published his *Méthode pour
apprendre à dessiner les passions*, which set out linear schemes for each emotion.
The book was soon translated, into Dutch in 1703, German in 1704, English in

INVID IA HI

59　DRAWN COPIES FROM THE FLAT

Pint. por Velazquez.   855   Dibux. por Goya.

Sacada y gravada del Quadro original de D. Diego Velazquez en que representa al vivo un
Enano del S. Phelipe IV. por D. Francisco Goya Pintor. Existe en el R.l Palacio de Madrid
Año de 1778.

37. Baccio Bandinelli (1493-1560); Italian
Study of two male nudes, after
Michelangelo's cartoon for the Battle of
Cascina; below, a slight sketch of a hand in
black chalk.
Inscribed *Michelangelo*. With the mark of
Count? Gelozzoi or Gelosi (Lugt 545)
Pen and ink and wash. 33 x 27.6 cm.
Ward-Jackson noted that 'According to
Vasari, Bandinelli was the most assiduous of
those Florentine artists who made Michelangelo's cartoon their study during the short
period when it was accessible to them,
before it was divided up, scattered and
destroyed. The two figures represented in
this drawing differ substantially from those
in any known preparatory studies by
Michelangelo and in later copies after the
Cartoon... There is no way of deciding
whether Bandinelli introduced these
variations or whether they are based on an
earlier preparatory study by Michelangelo.'
Bibl: Ward-Jackson I 31.

38. Francisco José Goya y Lucientes
(1746-1828); Spanish
The buffoon Diego de Acedo 'El Primo'
Drawing for a plate in the series of etchings
after Velázquez, reproduced with the
etching, 4th state, 1778.
The drawing is inscribed in ink *Pint. por
Valazquez. Dibux. por Goya*. The print is
inscribed *Sacada y gravada del Quadro
original de D.Diego Velasquez en que representa
al vivo un Enano del S. Phelipe IV. por D.
Francisco Goya Pintor. Existe en el R.l Palacio
de Madrid Año de 1778*.
Black chalk. 19 x 15 cm.;
etching 21.5 x 15.4 cm.
Goya issued seventeen prints after paintings
by Velázquez for which at least twelve
preparatory drawings are known. At the
time they were produced he was working for
the Santa Barbara tapestry factory under
the direction of Mengs who greatly admired

Velázquez and urged the younger painters
'not only to copy (his works) but above all to
imitate them'. Working on cartoons for
tapestries to decorate the royal residences,
Goya made his drawn copies of the
paintings, which had recently been installed
in the King's apartments of the Royal Palace
of Madrid, from the originals. The drawings
were used to provide guidelines for the
etching needle. First dampened, the
drawings were placed face down on the
prepared copper plates and run through the
printing press, so that the lines were
transferred in reverse on to the etching
grounds. (The process of printing the
finished plates on paper reversed the images
again so that the etchings were in the same
sense as the drawings.)
Bibl: P. Gassier, *The drawings of Goya*, 1975,
no. 29; L. Delteil, *Le peintre graveur illustré*,
vol. XIV, 1969, no. 19.

39. Jacques-Louis David (1748-1825);
French
Study of the head of St Michael, after a
detail from a painting by Guido Reni in
S. Maria della Concezione, Rome,
1775-1780
Inscribed by the artist *Colere noble et Elevee*;
inscribed in ink by the artist's sons Eugéne
and Jules *E.D.* and *J.D.*
Black Chalk. 15.5 x 14 cm.
Guido Reni's painting is derived from
Raphael's composition of the same subject
executed by Giulio Romano, now in the
Louvre in Paris. In spite of winning the
French Academy's 'Têtes d'expression'
competition in 1773, David stopped painting
when he arrived in Rome in 1775 because
he thought 'he drew badly, and did not have
good taste or know of what beauty consisted' and 'like a young student, set about
drawing eyes, ears, mouths, feet and hands
and made copies after the most beautiful
statues for a whole year. Anatomy was also
one of his chosen subjects.'
Bibl: Arlette Sérullaz, 'Dessins de Jacques-
Louis David', *La revue du Louvre et des
Musées de France*, 1980, pp. 100-105.

40. William Dyce, RA (1806-1864); British
A figure copied from a fresco by
Domenichino at the Monastery of Grotta
Ferrata, 1844
Pencil and water-colour. 36 x 23 cm.
Having obtained the commission to paint
one of the frescoes in the House of Lords in
London, Dyce went to Italy to refresh his
memory of Renaissance fresco. He made
diagrams and detailed coloured notes, many
of which were subsequently published in
'Observations on Fresco Painting', printed
as Appendix IV to the *Sixth Report of the
Commissioners on the Fine Arts*, 1846. He must
have made many such studies as this
drawing.
Bibl: Marcia Pointon, *William Dyce 1806-
1864*, 1979, p. 90.

41. School of Jacopo Tintoretto (Jacopo Robusti) (1518-1594); Italian
Studies from Michelangelo's lost group of Samson slaying two Philistines
With the collector's mark of Sir J. Reynolds (Lugt 2364)
Black chalk heightened with white on faded blue paper. 36.1 x 28.3 cm.
Ward-Jackson comments that 'At least fifteen other similar studies by Tintoretto and his school are known. Tintoretto is known to have drawn regularly from sculpture, and his studio was stocked with models and casts. This study may have been made from a cast of Michelangelo's group or from one of the small bronze or terracotta versions...'
Bibl: Ward-Jackson I 339.

42. Domenico Gargiulo (Micco Spadaro)
(?1612-? before 1665 or possibly 1679);
Italian
Six studies from different viewpoints of an
armless female statue
Inscribed *Micco Spadaro*
Pen and ink. 18 x 25 cm.
Spadaro was a painter who specialized in
inserting figures into architectural settings.
Bibl: Ward-Jackson II 702.

1734 and Italian in 1751, and gave rise to numerous more elaborate works based upon it. Soon drawing became identified with the theoretical and 'intellectual' aspects of painting, and colour with the more craftsmanlike qualities, with the result that drawing was the more highly valued, and became the medium through which the student familiarised himself with visual perfection.

The 'Rules and Orders, relating to the School of Design' of the Royal Academy made clear the important part drawing – particularly drawing from the round – played in the progress of its students: 'Each student, who offers himself for admission... shall present a drawing or model from some plaister cast to the Keeper, and if he thinks him properly qualified he shall be permitted to make a drawing or model from some cast in the Royal Academy, which if approved of by the Keeper and Visitor for the time being, shall be laid before the Council for their confirmation, which obtained he shall receive his letter of

43. Probably by Antonio Domenico
Gabbiani (1652-1726); Italian
Study after an antique bas-relief
A youth, perhaps a Meleager, (his head,
hands and one leg missing) seated beside a
dog
Red chalk. 37.4 x 23.3 cm.
From late in the fifteenth century artists
had excitedly attended excavations in their
search for newly-discovered antique
sculptures and reliefs, as models of excel-
lence to guide their own creativity. Casts of
the more famous works soon became
available in centres of study. This drawing
of a damaged relief would have been a
routine exercise for a seventeenth-century
painter such as Gabbiani, who attended the
Florentine Academy in Rome.
Bibl: Ward-Jackson II 700.

44. Anonymous
Plan and elevation of a capital in the front of the church at Terracina. *c.* 1780
Pen and ink and water-colour. 59.5 x 42 cm.
This careful study was acquired by the Victoria & Albert Museum as part of a collection of eighty-two similar drawings of Roman capitals in 1880: all intended for use as models for art students to follow.

45. Filippo Agricola (1776-1857); Italian
Study of the Laocoon
One of six studies from antique sculpture
Red chalk. 38 x 29.5 cm.
The Laocoon was found in the Baths of Titus in Rome in 1506, and made a great impression on Michelangelo and his school, who studied it closely. As time progressed the number of antique sculptures considered suitable as models to copy diminished, but the Laocoon remained one of the most valued.

Agricola was a student at the Accademia di S. Luca and made many studies both after the Antique and from sixteenth century works. He was considered one of the most able Roman painters, and as such received many important commissions, including portraits.

admission as a Student in the Royal Academy. Where he shall continue to draw after the plaister, till the Keeper and Visitor... judge him qualified to draw after the living models...'[9] Thomas Stothard, librarian to the Royal Academy from 1814 to 1834 is remembered for his insistence that 'merely drawing the figure from the living subject at the Academy was not enough; the student who does so, without being prepared by previous study from the antique, will be apt to depict nature too much after the Dutch School, in vulgar or common forms, wanting that poetic grace or beauty in which the Greek sculptors exceeded all others, of any age or country.'[10] The popular artist William Frith, who disliked

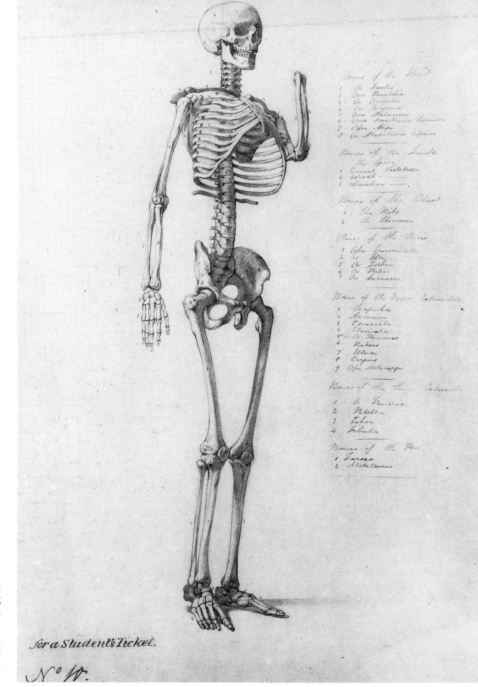

for a Student's Ticket.

Nº W.

46. William Edward Frost, RA (1810-1877);
British
Study of a human skeleton
Signed *W.E. Frost* (partially erased).
Inscribed with notes and *for a Student's
Ticket* and *No. 10*
Pencil. 52.5 x 36.3 cm.
Frost studied at Henry Sass's School and at
the Royal Academy in London (this drawing
may have been prepared to help his
admission to the Academy). Skeltons and
écorché casts (showing the musculature of a
body) were standard props in workshops
and art academies from the seventeenth
century onwards.

47. Sir (Samuel) Luke Fildes, KCVO, RA
(1843-1927); British
Study of a plaster cast foot
Signed and dated *L. Fildes* and *S.L. Fildes
Dec 1st 1863* with the blind stamp of the
Science and Art Department, inscribed
15438
Black and white chalk on buff paper
39.4 x 40 cm.
Fildes drew this study shortly after entering
the British National Art Training School
(now the Royal College of Art) with a
scholarship, after three years training at a
provincial school of art. At first British
state-run schools, in opposition to the
Academy Schools did not permit drawing
from casts although the syllabus was,
nevertheless, based on drawing from other
approved models. By the time the Schools of
Design had evolved into the Schools of Art,
such academic training was, as is shown by
this exercise, encouraged.

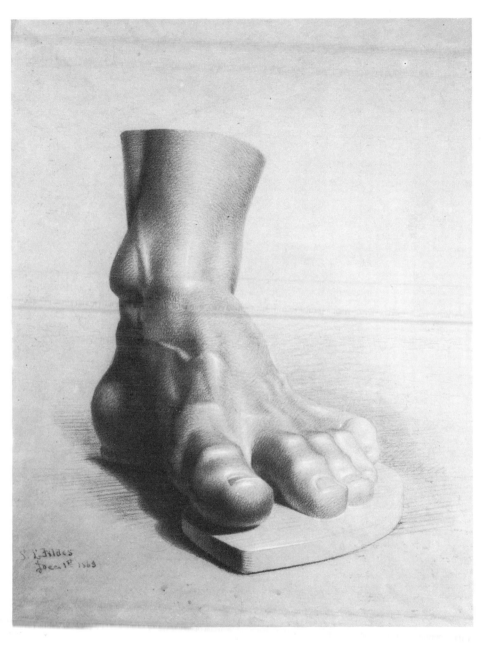

the prescribed curriculum, accepted that it was the only way into the life class
and that it had certain merits: 'Consider the quality of mind and body requisite
for an artistic career – long and severe study from antique statues, from five to
eight hours every day; then many months hard work from life, with attendance
at lectures ... general reading to be attended to also – all before painting
is attempted.'[11]

48. Bartolomeo Passarotti (1529-1592);
Italian
Five studies of nudes
Inscribed *Baccio Bandinelli*
Pen and ink. 41.9 x 26 cm.
The drawing of these figures shows the
influence of Michelangelo.
Bibl: Ward-Jackson I 242.

49. John Constable, RA (1776-1837); British
Study of a seated male nude. *c.* 1800
Charcoal heightened with white chalk, on
brown toned paper. 53 x 41 cm.
Constable attended the Royal Academy
Schools from 1799. His biographer wrote
that he had 'seen no studies made by
Constable at the Academy from the antique,
but many chalk drawings and oil paintings
from the living model, all of which have
great breadth of light and shade, though
they are sometimes defective in outline.'
Constable continued to draw from the nude
throughout his career, though his exhibited
works were mainly landscapes.
Bibl: C.R. Leslie, *Memoirs of the Life of John
Constable, RA*, ed. A. Shirley, 1937, p. 13.
G. Reynolds, *Catalogue of the Constable
Collection*, 1973, no. 17.

In 1837 the first state-run British school, The London School of Design, was opened and its curriculum also stressed the importance of drawing. Shortly afterwards *The Drawing Book of the Government School of Design* by the painter and educationalist William Dyce (see fig. 40) was issued, stating in the introduction that the book was 'in the first place to serve as an elementary drawing-book for schools, and in particular for those schools whose ultimate purpose is to educate young persons in the art of inventing and executing patterns and designs for the various branches of ornamented manufacture; and in the second place, to be a hand-book of ornamental art for the use and guidance of manufacturers and pattern draughtsmen.' The course of instruction 'affords materials for three kinds of practical study necessary to the ornamentist viz., that of geometrical drawing, of the drawing of linear ornament by the hand, and of artistical imitation of solid objects...' while making 'the attainment of manual dexterity a means of acquaintance of the established and classical forms of decorative art.' Despite this invitation to art to serve the needs of the machine, greater emphasis came to be put on the artist's individuality. The attitude that was later to be expressed by Gauguin gained ground: 'To know how to draw does not mean to draw well. Let us examine that famous science of

50. John Gibson, RA (1776-1866); British
Écorché study of a horse. *c.* 1815
Pencil. 22.5 x 35.8 cm.
Gibson was a sculptor, who began working
in marble before he received any formal
training. His work was noticed by the
banker and connoisseur William Roscoe,
who encouraged him to copy works by
Renaissance artists from his collection, and,
as the artist recalled, to study anatomy
'from the subject itself.' He continues
'Knowing what an anatomist Michel Angelo
was, I was most eager to begin. Dr Vose of
Liverpool was giving lectures on anatomy to
young surgeons at that time, and he
generously admitted me into his school
gratis. With his instruction, and close
devotion to the dissecting-room, I became
well versed in the construction of the
human body, and could detect at a glance
any anatomical error in a work of art.'
Although this study is likely to have been
made from a cast rather than a dissected
animal, the anatomy of the horse merited
almost as much attention from artists in the
eighteenth and nineteenth centuries as that
of the human body.
Bibl: *Life of John Gibson, RA, Sculptor*,
ed. Lady Eastlake, 1870. pp 33, 34.

51. William Mulready, RA (1786-1863);
British
Study of a seated male nude
Signed *WM* and inscribed *Kensington Life
Academy, 2 Dec 1859. A.L. Egg placed the
figure*
Black and red chalk. 34 x 55.5 cm.
On November 11th 1857 Richard Redgrave
(the compiler of Redgrave's *Dictionary of
artists in Britain*) commented in his diary 'I
believe Mulready is seventy-three, and yet
there he is, hard at work at the 'Life', like
any young student. He is not only attending
as Visitor, and drawing at the Royal
Academy, but he is one of a party who meet
three times a week at Ansdell's for studying
from the life.' The Victoria & Albert
Museum possesses nearly one hundred of
his studies of nudes, ranging in date from
1805 to 1862. They do not relate to specific
paintings but are rather an entity in
themselves. When they were exhibited
together at Gore House in 1853, Queen
Victoria was much impressed by them.
Bibl: A. Rorimer, *Drawings by William
Mulready*, 1972, no. 2.

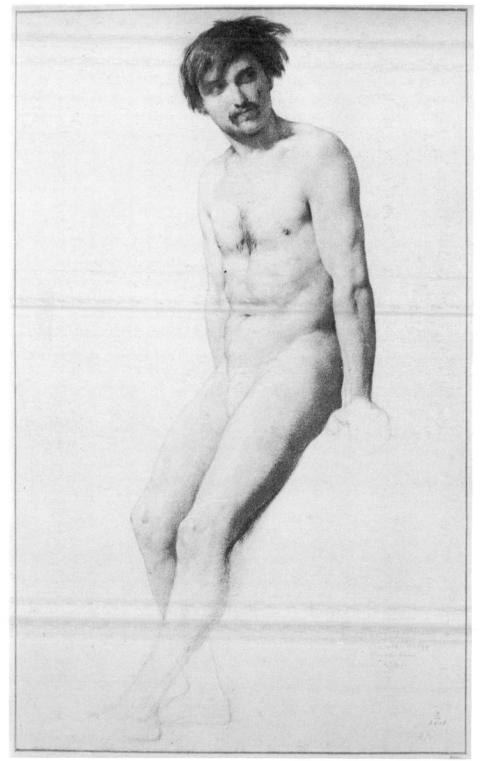

52. Henry Tonks, FRCS (1862-1937);
British
Three studies on one sheet of a female nude
Black and red chalk on pale blue paper.
43 x 28 cm.
Tonks had considerable importance as a
teacher, particularly during his Professor-
ship at the Slade School of Art in London
from 1917 to 1930. He emphasized the
importance of drawing for a painter, writing:
'Italy, up to near the end of the sixteenth
century will always be the best school for all
those who want to learn what drawing can
explain... As it is by drawings that we make
our records of form, its importance cannot
be exaggerated. A school of painting in
which drawing is not taught and drawing
dissociated with painting is not worthy of
the name of school. When the student
begins to paint he will soon perceive the
relation of drawing to paint.'
Bibl: J. Hare, *The Life of Henry Tonks*, 1939,
pp 172, 173.

53. Fernand Léger (1881-1955); French
Study of a seated female nude.
Signed and dated *FL08*
Pen and ink. 25 x 12 cm.
Analysis of the human form was central to Cubism.

draughtsmanship we hear so much about. Every Prix de Rome has that science at his finger-tips; so have the competitors who came in last...'[12]

But the opposing view expressed by Van Gogh in a letter of 1884 to his brother also remained common: 'I have bought myself a very beautiful book on anatomy...It was in fact very expensive, but it will be of use to me all my life, for it is very good. I have also what they use at the Ecole de Beaux-Arts, and what they use in Antwerp... The key to many things is in thorough knowledge of the human body, but it costs money to learn it. Besides, I am quite sure that colour, that chiaroscuro, that perspective, that tone and that drawing, in short, everything has fixed laws which one must and can study, like chemistry or algebra. This is far from being the easiest view and one who says, "Oh, one must know it all instinctively" takes it very easy indeed. If that were enough. But it isn't enough, for even if one knows it ever so much by instinct, that is just the reason to try ever so hard to pass from instinct to reason.'[13] Academic training, with its emphasis on drawing, has continued to be valued as a good grounding.

Only during this century has such a formalized curriculum been discarded but drawing has, nevertheless, continued to play an important part in art school teaching. At the Bauhaus, the most influential training centre for artists and designers, Kandinsky held 'analytical drawing' classes as part of the preliminary course which all students attended. Referring to them, he wrote: 'Drawing instruction is a training towards perception, exact observation and exact presentation not of the outward appearances of an object, but of its constructive elements, its lawful forces – tensions, which can be discovered in given objects and of the logical structures of same – education toward clear observation and clear rendering of the contexts, whereby surface phenomena are an introductory step towards the three-dimensional.'[14] Even better known is Klee's belief in the value of drawing. In his *Pedagogical Sketchbook*, he examined seeing and being through a line in action, encouraging his students towards 'a free creation of abstract forms which supersede didactic principles with a new naturalness, the naturalness of the work'.[15]

54. Andrea del Verrocchio (1435-1488); Italian
Design for a monument in the form of a covered bowl, with a personification of Justice on the cover and other figures
With the collector's mark of Sir T. Lawrence (Lugt 2445)
Black chalk, partly gone over in pen and ink and wash. 27.3 x 17.5 cm.
Bibl: Ward-Jackson I 18.

DRAWING AS IMAGINATION

55. Francesco di Simone (1437-1493);
Italian
Design for an altar
Inscribed within a cartouche in the border
Desiderio da Settignano scult
Black chalk, pen and ink and wash,
heightened with white, on paper partly
tinted pink, 44.5 x 28 cm
It has been suggested that this is one of
seven different designs (two others of which
are in the collection of the Victoria & Albert
Museum), made in an attempt to solve the
difficult problem of combining a tabernacle
with an altar. The drawing is mounted in a
border decorated with trophies, as were
drawings in Vasari's collection, and it was
no doubt Vasari who wrote Desiderio's
name in the cartouche.
Bibl: Ward-Jackson I 2. *See* Plate XI.

Even drawings produced in a drawing office following another's instructions owe something to the draughtsman's interpretation, and so could be termed works of the imagination. But the illustrations to this chapter concentrate firstly on drawings (arranged in chronological order) which show the artist or designer thinking on paper, his mind working in graphic form without consciously intending a finished work of art (figs. 54-67), and then on drawings intended as ends in themselves, to be valued as expressions of the artist's vision and imagination as much as for what they depict (figs. 68-80). The aim is to look at the part drawing has played in the creation of works of art, artefacts and machines and to study the relationship between this role of drawing as an imaginative process, and the development of drawing as a highly prized artistic form in its own right.

Although not all artists and designers have made drawings many have found that drawing helps the development of an idea in much the same way as thoughts can be clarified by being put into words. A humble design for drinking glasses by Philip Webb (fig. 63) shows their shapes being formulated in the designer's mind; the studies of balletic groups by Gontcharova (fig. 65) show her trying out the costumes and scenery in a succession of formations. And no lesser artist than Michelangelo is said to have destroyed many of his preliminary sketches because he did not want posterity to see the extent of his labours. The attitude expressed by Henry Moore in an interview for the *New Yorker* is typical: 'Drawing is a means of finding your way about things, and a way of experiencing, more quickly than sculpture allows, certain tryouts and attempts.'[16] The act of converting an idea into lines and other marks on paper often excites the mind and frees the imagination, encouraging the flow of creative thought.

Obviously not all those who have made drawings have followed the same procedure, step by step. Nevertheless drawings made to work out solutions to problems as varied as the design of the Crystal Palace for the Great Exhibition of 1851 by Sir Joseph Paxton (fig. 61) or the composition of a picture by Canaletto (fig. 59) or the design of an automobile body by Sir Alec Issigonis (fig. 67) have certain features in common. Such drawings are likely, for example, to include sketches of the overall layout or shape, drawings which study the relationship between the parts, for example proportion and perspective studies, and drawings which break the design down into its components. Annibale

56. Pier Francesco Morazzone
(Mazzucchelli) (1571 or 1573-1626); Italian
An angel in flight
Inscribed in ink *Morazone*
Black chalk with white on pale brown paper
tinted pink; squared in black chalk
26.4. x 25.7 cm.
A study for one of the angels holding scrolls
in the fresco of the 'Ascent to Calvary' in
the thirty-sixth chapel on the Sacro Monte
di Varallo.
Bibl: Ward-Jackson I 200.

57. Sir Peter Paul Rubens (1577-1640);
Flemish
Studies for the tapestry 'The Death of
Decius Mus'
The head, shoulders and left arm (three
variants) of the warrior who transfixes the
consul with a downward thrust of his lance;
the left arm, holding a sword, and the right
forearm, holding the reins, of the horseman
on the right; and the right arm of a
struggling figure under the horses' hooves.
c. 1617
Black chalk, heightened with white
41.2 x 31 cm.
'The Death of Decius Mus' was one of the
tapestry series commissioned from Rubens
by a group of Genoese noblemen in 1617,
which depicted events in the life of the
Roman consul Decius Mus. While the
paintings which Rubens made for the series
are now in the Liechtenstein collection at
Vaduz, the actual cartoons, which were
presumably in tempera on paper, are
missing. On this sheet of vigorously drawn
studies the artist experiments freely with
various arm movements which are key
features in the dramatic action.
Bibl: J.S. Held, *Rubens, Selected Drawings*,
1959 no. 89.

58. Sir Anthony Van Dyck (1599-1641);
Flemish
Christ crowned with thorns
Inscribed with the mark of the collection of
Jonathan Richardson, Jr. (Lugt 2170)
Pen and ink and brown wash
23.3 x 20.7 cm.

Van Dyck painted two versions of 'Christ
crowned with thorns', the original of which
was in the Kaiser Friedrich Museum in
Berlin until its destruction in 1945. The
second is in the Museo del Prado, Madrid.
This drawing is one of several studies for
the whole composition made in Antwerp
before 1621, and other studies from the
series are in the collections of the Amsterdam Historical Museum, the Musée du
Petit Palais and the Louvre in Paris. This is
an early study which is characterized by the
dramatic treatment of its subject, achieved
through free and incisive draughtsmanship,
bold use of chiaroscuro, and a compositional
structure in which a series of pronounced
diagonals leads from the bottom left of the
image to the upper right, through the
inclined body of Christ. In this and other
studies, Van Dyck was able to experiment
with the content, structure and mood of his
final painting (ultimately the subject is
treated with far more restraint and
stability); the drawings are thus the
projection of his thought-process as well as
essays to be valued in their own right.
Bibl: J.R. Martin & G. Feigenbaum, *Van
Dyck as Religious Artist*, 1979, no. 11.

XII Francesco di Simone. *See* fig. 55.

DESIDERIO DA SETTIGNANO SCVLT.

XII Anonymous. *See* fig. 72.

XIII. Francesco Guardi (1712-1793); Italian
A Venetian villa terminating an avenue, with figures
On the back, a rough sketch of a regatta
Pen and ink and wash. 28 x 39.7 cm.
Guardi was a prolific draughtsman, making preparatory studies for paintings, and sketching
groups with or without settings, which might or might not be used in future compositions.
He also drew the more or less topographical scenes which provided foreign travellers with
souvenirs and the *capricci*, combining invented and existing architectural and landscape
motifs, which appealed to his countrymen. This drawing probably portrays the garden and
exterior of a specific villa in Venice but the freedom with which the scene is handled links it
with some of his more romantic visions.
Bibl: Ward-Jackson II 1028.

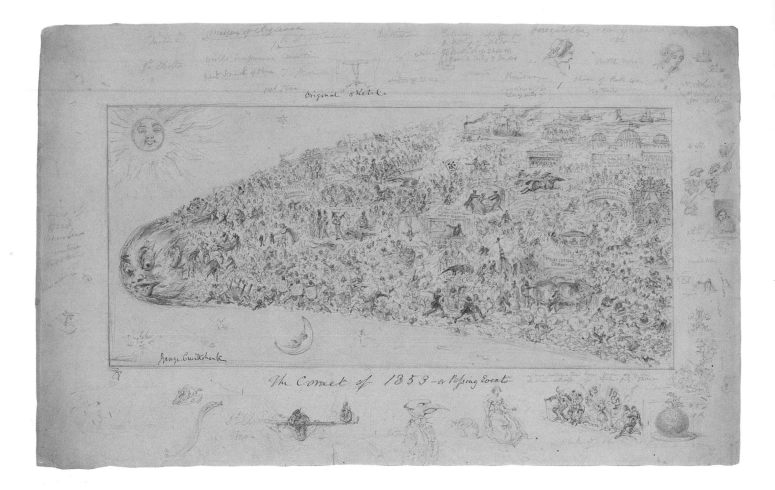

George Cruikshank

The Comet of 1853 — or Passing Events

59. Antonio Canal (called Canaletto)
(1697-1768); Italian
St Mark's, Venice, the interior, looking
across from the south to the north transept.
Preparatory study for the drawing in the
Kunsthalle at Hamburg. *c.* 1766
Inscribed with notes
Pen and ink over red and black chalk
36.2 x 30.8 cm.
The finished drawing corresponds closely
with this prepartory work, but is enlivened
by the use of wash, by the addition of
numerous figures and by a more exact
delineation of detail. The preparatory
drawing is interesting as an example of
Canaletto's way of working. Most of the
straight lines are drawn with a ruler in black
chalk and afterwards gone over freehand in
ink. The vanishing point is marked with a
spot of ink just to the right of the
sarcophagus against the end wall of the
transept, and many of the vanishing lines
are still visible, lightly drawn in black chalk.
If the drawing is turned on its right side,
another sketch can be faintly seen.
Bibl: W. Vitzthum, 'A drawing by
Canaletto', *Burlington Magazine*, vol. XCIX,
1957, p. 276, pl. 40; Ward-Jackson II 953.

Carracci, describing the process which led up to the painting of his decoration
in the Farnesina in Bologna, wrote: 'First one imagines a pose, different from
other people's inventions, but beautiful, suitable to the situation, pleasing, and
comprehensible: and this he sketches several times. Next one draws details –
this leg, that arm – from the model, in correct attitude. Finally one brings all
this together into the cartoon...'[17] The first part of such a process can be seen at
work in Rubens' drawing for the 'Death of Decius Mus' tapestry (fig. 57).
While the philosophy behind contemporary design may be very different,
workshop practice is curiously similar. In the case of designing an automobile,
for example, drawings may be made to work out the appearance of and the
relationship between such components as the fins, the hood, the headlights and

XIV George Cruikshank. *See* fig. 62.

Interno della Chiesa di SS. Pietro e Paolo e due figure che dimostrano la funzione che anno fatto nel Pontificale del Papa Pio VI. l'anno 1782. a Venezia.

60. Francesco Guardi (1712-1793); Italian
The interior of the church of SS Giovanni e
Paolo at Venice, on 16 May 1782, when
Pope Pius VI celebrated Mass there
Inscribed in ink (probably in Guardi's hand)
*Interno della Chiesa di SS Gio e Paolo e sue
Figure che dimostrano la Fonzione che anno
fatto nel Pontificale del Papa Pio VI. L'anno
1782 a Venezia.*
Pen and ink and wash over black chalk
58.1 x 55 cm.
Guardi was commissioned by Pietro
Edwards, Inspector of Fine Arts to the
Republic, to paint four pictures to
commemorate the Pope's visit to Venice.
This drawing is a nearly actual-size study
for the architectural setting of one of them.
Containing no figures, it was presumably
made in the church either before or after the
Papal Mass had been celebrated. Two other
drawings for the composition are known.
One is a small 'impressionist' view of the
scene with figures and architecture, perhaps
drawn during the Mass, and the other is a
large study of the disposition of the figures
removed from their setting, probably drawn
in the artist's studio when the details of the
composition were being worked out. Two
paintings of the subject are known; both
have the same viewpoint as this drawing but
one shows more of the church to the right
and neither includes the view of the dome.
Bibl: A. Morassi, *Guardi, tutti i disegni di
Antonio, Francesco e Giacomo Guardi*, 1976,
no. 271; Ward-Jackson II 1031.

61. Sir Joseph Paxton (1801-1865); British
First sketch for the Great Exhibition
building. 1850, built 1851
Pen and ink on pink blotting paper
39.4 x 28 cm.
This rough sketch of a cross-section and
elevation reminiscent of Paxton's lily house
at Chatsworth was the germ of the design
for the Great Exhibition building. Drawn on
a blotter during a meeting of the disci-
plinary board of the Midland Railway, over
which Paxton was presiding, it was, quite
literally, a 'doodle'. But within a week
Paxton had worked it into the comprehensive proposal which was to be adopted in
preference to the scheme put forward by the
Exhibition Committee.

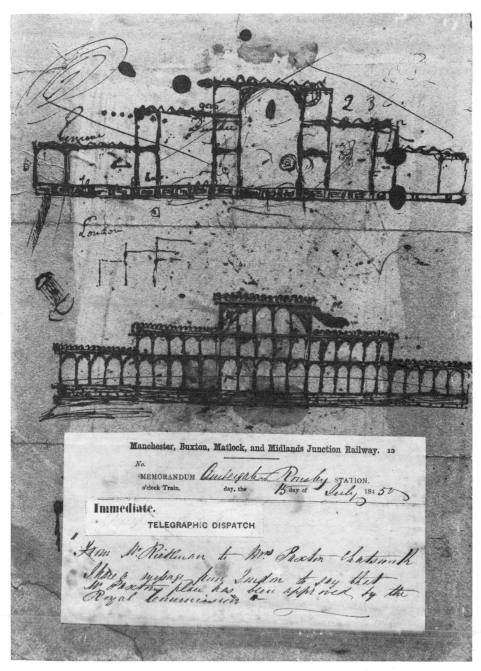

62. George Cruikshank (1792-1878); British
Sketch for the etching 'Passing events, or
the Tail of the Comet of 1853', an
illustration to *George Cruikshank's Magazine*,
published London, 1 January 1854, no. 1
Signed in ink *George Cruikshank*.
Inscribed in ink *The Comet of 1853 – or
Passing Events. Original sketch*, and in pencil
around the margin with various notes.
Pencil and water-colour
Size of sheet 30.3 x 48.5 cm. (detail)
In this humorous drawing, Cruikshank
included references to the events which
epitomised the year 1853, for example the
Peace Conference, the war between Russia
and Turkey, the naval review at Ports-
mouth, the Smithfield Cattle Show, Guy
Fawkes and Derby Day. He used the area
around the margin to work out individual
images for possible inclusion in the densely
populated trail of the comet.
See Plate XIV.

(ii) Glastonbury or Canterbury, mid 10th
century
Miscellaneous texts and Gregory the Great,
Pastoral Care
Christ, beardless, with cross-shaft and book
Pen and red ink on vellum. 32.8 x 23.7 cm.
This splendid drawing is not related to the
surrounding text, and it is clear from the
layout of the page that the drawing was
made first and the text written round it.

the roof-line.

The degree of finish of drawings related to work in progress varies according
to the nature of the problem and the individual artist's or designer's method of
working. Nevertheless, general layouts tend to be roughly sketched, as in Van
Dyck's sketch for the composition of the painting 'Christ crowned with thorns'
(fig. 58), while the various components are more often precisely drawn, as in
Seurat's meticulous study of anchors (fig. 64) or Morazzone's flying angel (fig.
56). Some drawings may include detailed and sketchy work on one sheet. Areas
required to put a detail in context may be drawn roughly, while the particular
problem with which the artist is concerned may be worked more elaborately:
this appears to be the case in the Verrocchio drawing (fig. 54).

It is thought that drawings only began to be made as ends in themselves early
in the Renaissance. There exist, nevertheless, drawings on the flyleaves of
Mediaeval manuscripts which have no known purpose and which give the
impression of being spontaneous expressions of the artist's imagination (fig. ii).
Even after that period it is often difficult to tell if a drawing was made as a step in
the production of something else or as an end in itself, and in reality the
distinction may be blurred. Leonardo wrote: 'You will be glad to have by you a
little book of leaves prepared with ground bone, and to note down notions in it
with a silverpoint... when it is full, keep it to serve your future plans, and take
another and carry on with it.'[18]

Many drawings are made solely out of some sort of graphic curiosity but

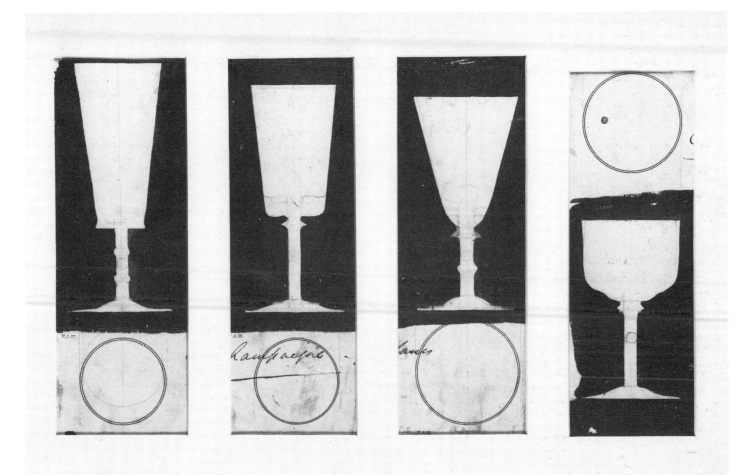

63. Philip Webb (1831-1915); British
Four designs for champagne glasses
Designed for James Powell and Sons,
Whitefriars. *c.* 1861
Pencil, pen and wash. Each *c.* 25.5 x 19 cm.
A variety of shapes for each glass was tried out
in pencil and the selected form was picked out
in silhouette against a black ground.

nevertheless they become part of the artist's repertoire and thus available to be used in some other way should the need arise. Drawing was a vital and continuous part of Rembrandt's life. While he did make sketches in connection with specific compositions, the majority were almost involuntary products of his inner vision or, as in the case of figure 69, of his response to his surroundings. Nevertheless, although made for their own sakes, his sketches were filed in his studio under headings such as 'animals', 'figures' or 'landscapes', so that they could be called on to provide inspiration for future paintings or prints. Artists such as Watteau (fig. 71) also deliberately kept his sketches and consulted them regularly for visual ideas. A number of Watteau's contemporaries recorded that he was more pleased with his drawings than his paintings. The picture dealer, Gersaint, wrote: 'He found it a greater pleasure to draw than to paint. I have often seen him out of temper with himself because he was unable to convey in painting the truth and brilliance that he could express with his pencil'[19] and the Comte de Caylus recalled 'The exercise of drawing had infinite charms for him and although sometimes the figure on

64. Georges Pierre Seurat (1859-1891);
French
Anchors
Study for 'The Channel at Gravelines,
Evening'. 1890
Conté crayon. 23.7 x 31.5 cm.
During his short life Seurat made over seven hundred drawings. Some of these are independent works while others are studies for paintings, and demonstrate the methodical way in which he built up his compositions; thirty drawings are recorded for one of his major exhibition pieces. The three surviving drawings for 'The Channel at Gravelines, Evening' are typical of such studies. The two others consist of overall views of the scene from which elements are extracted and combined in the painting, whereas this drawing shows the form of one element, the pair of anchors, being explored. The shape they make is refined and their tonal value related to the surrounding space.
Bibl: C.M. de Hauke, *Seurat et son oeuvre*, 1961, no.698.

65. Natalia Sergeevna Gontcharova (1881-1964); Russian
Two designs for choreography, showing groups of female dancers for the ballet *Les Noces*, with words and music by Stravinsky, first produced at the Gaieté-Lyrique Theatre, Paris, 13 July 1923
Pen and indian ink
Size of sheets 27 x 21 cm.
Stravinsky's *Les Noces* was inspired by the rites and ceremonies traditionally associated with a Russian peasant wedding. When Diaghilev decided to produce it as a ballet, he invited Bronislava Nijinska to do the choreography and Gontcharova the settings and costumes. After much discussion, Gontcharova was persuaded by Nijinska to abandon her original richly coloured designs in favour of a set which, in its stark austerity, better reflected the mood of the choreography. These drawings are examples of the choreographic groups, some of them highly sculptural, which Gontcharova also created for the ballet.

which he happened to be at work was not a study undertaken with any particular purpose in view, he had the greatest imaginable difficulty in tearing himself away from it.'[20] Figures from the same drawings appear in painted compositions executed by Watteau several years apart. Examples of artists finding inspiration in casual sketches abound: John Constable made some pencil sketches, including figure 75, on a visit to Stonehenge in 1820, and returned to them when he decided to paint an exhibition piece on the theme some fifteen years later (plate XVII). Toulouse-Lautrec sketched obsessively in cafés and nightclubs and, as is the case with figure 78, sometimes used these records of a fleeting moment as the basis for fully worked-out compositions. Gauguin also used his drawings (fig. 77) as a personal and private source for his paintings.

There is no doubt that drawings on loose sheets rather than in notebooks began to be preserved increasingly during the fifteenth century. To begin with they were kept by artists as patterns to follow, but from that practice developed that of masters giving departing apprentices a sheet of drawing for remembrance and so drawings soon became personal tokens of esteem. It is recorded that in 1508 Raphael sent a drawing of the *Nativity* to Francia asking for a *Judith* in return and Michelangelo is known to have made drawings for Vittoria Colonna. As artists became increasingly self-conscious and broke away from the guilds, and the public became more aware of the artist's individual place in society, more graphic jottings – drawings showing the working-out of ideas – were preserved both by artists and collectors. The artist and biographer, Vasari, is thought to have formed the first collection of drawings created from a

historical point of view, in which each artist, whatever Vasari thought of the quality of their drawings, received equal treatment: the drawing by Francesco di Simone (fig. 55) is from Vasari's collection. Cosimo de Medici was one of the first lay collectors to develop a passion for drawings. During the 1560s he began assembling an album of finished works by 150 great masters, selecting drawings which had been made for one reason or another as ends in themselves (though as the note to figure 68 shows, they were not all appreciated by a later generation).

By the seventeenth century drawings were in such demand that speculators bought the contents of studios wholesale in order to sell the drawings off slowly, their value increasing with the passage of time. Marks identifying collectors became common and drawings began to be mounted individually with gold and tinted borders instead of being stored in albums. Connoisseurly sensibility and discrimination developed among critics and collectors, and the importance of drawings in appreciating an individual artist's work began to be recognised. This is reflected in the continuing interest of scholars in the reattribution of drawings to particular artists: figure 54 is a typical example of a drawing of which the quality has in itself led to speculation about its authorship.

The drawing shows a design for a monument, and it is unsigned. In his *Catalogue of Italian Drawings in the Victoria & Albert Museum*, Ward-Jackson plotted the history of its attributions as follows: 'our drawing, described as a design for a chalice, was ascribed to Leonardo da Vinci in the Woodburn sale. It was first attributed to Verrocchio by Meder and Steinmann in 1928, according to a note in the Department [at the Victoria & Albert Museum]. Clark tentatively suggested the name of Benedetto da Maiano, but the other writers mentioned in the bibliography have either accepted Verrocchio as the author or given the drawing to Credi, his favourite pupil. The protagonists of Credi are Berenson and Dalli Regoli. The latter includes the sheet in her catalogue of Credi's drawings, but admits that he may have worked over a drawing of Verrocchio. Berenson also acknowledges the influence of Verrocchio. Moller deduces from the presence of the Lion of St Mark that the drawing is that design for a Doge's tomb which Vasari says belonged to Vincenzo Borghini; and he argues from the charge of a fess on one of the heraldic shields that the Doge was Andrea Vendramin, who died in 1478, but had no monument until after 1490. This hypothesis is supported by Passavant, who dates the drawing about 1485, and by Seymour. It is certainly possible that Verrocchio may have had such a commission while he was working on the Colleoni monument in Venice.' Such concern and enthusiasm is a measure of the worth of great master drawings and an indication of the problems facing art historians in ascribing authorship.

By the eighteenth century the passion for drawings had resulted in a market for distinct types. Some artists, like Greuze (plate XVI), specialized in the portrayal of the emotions, while others catered for the tourists' demand for souvenirs. Topographical views, such as Guardi's villa in plate XIII, were sought after by some, while others, including the Scottish visitor to Rome drawn by Ingres early in the nineteenth century (fig. 74), liked to see their own features in front of a 'view'. There was a vogue too for architectural *capricci* such

66. David Hockney (born 1937); British
2nd Dignitary. Sketch for oil painting
'A grand procession of Dignitaries painted
in the Semi-Egyptian Style'. 1961
Signed and dated *DH '61*
Charcoal and orange chalk on ochre paper
60.7 x 45.6 cm.
The subject of the painting was indirectly
inspired by a poem by the Greek poet
Constantine Cavafy, 'Waiting for the
Barbarians'.

By 1961 Hockney was already interested in
the style of Egyptian painting, and the way it
was governed by a rigid set of rules which
allowed the artist little individualism of
expression, and he created this work in a 'semi-
Egyptian style'. Thus the three dignitaries are
shown in the most characteristic Egyptian
fashion, with different parts of their bodies
viewed from set angles (the legs in profile and
the torso from the front, for example), highly
stylised and two-dimensional. But Hockney
creates a *double-entendre* by investing each
figure with a second, inner figure. The sketch,
although it is not very close to the final version
of the 2nd Dignitary, shows clearly the artist's
intention of playing on the ambiguity of inner
and outer self.
Bibl: Whitechapel Gallery, *David Hockney,
Paintings, Prints and Drawings 1960-1970*,
1970, nos. 61, 10.

XV Canaletto. *See* fig. 73.

XVI. Jean-Baptiste Greuze (1726-1805);
French
Girl's head, the face with an expression
of pain
Black chalk with traces of white heightening
on grey paper. 28.3 x 20.4 cm.
A constant and characteristic feature of
Greuze's art is his exploitation of gesture
and facial expression. This reflects his own
ceaseless observation and intense involvement with his subjects, and is also a means
whereby he engages the attention and
sympathy of the beholder. He made a great
many studies of expression, some in preparation for specific paintings, and others,
like this sketch, without a conscious end in
view. Greuze's *têtes d'expression* became
sought after by collectors, and were widely
copied from prints made after them.

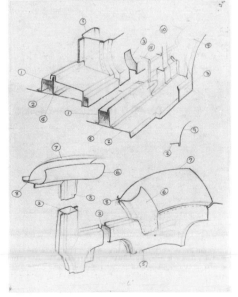

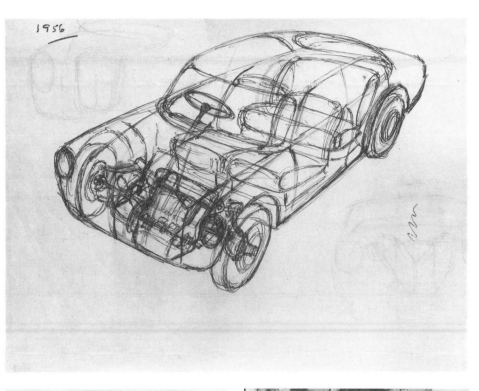

1956

67. Sir Alec Issigonis, CBE, FRS
(born 1906); British
Four sketches related to automobile design
a. Design thoughts for the dashboard area of
the Morris Minor. Inscribed with notes.
Felt-tip pen. Size of sheet 25.3 x 33 cm.
b. First concept of front-wheel drive,
transverse-engine vehicle. Dated *1956*
Ballpoint pen and pencil.
Size of sheet 32.9 x 25.3 cm.
c. Morris Minor body design details.
Numbered with key and inscribed with
measurement.
Pencil. 32.9 x 25.3 cm.
d. Drawing for test rig work. Inscribed *Means
of communication with the engineers shop. For
test rig work,* and with working notes.
Black and blue felt-tip pen on newspaper.
Sheet folded to 17 x 34.7 cm.

This group shows the importance of drawing
as a tool in the manufacture of an automobile,
both as a means of working out its design and
as a means of communication between the
different people involved. Of his sketches Sir
Alec has said: 'My doodles and sketches are
not the work of an academic engineer. They
represent many years of design study in
attempts to produce the best value for money
in the field of small car design. The engineer
who cannot draw cannot communicate his
thinking to his colleagues and to those who
have to translate his ideas into practical
reality.' The last drawing in this group was
made by Issigonis in order to demonstrate the
ephemeral nature of many of his sketches.

69. Rembrandt Harmensz van Rijn
(1606-1669); Dutch
View over flat country, with Amsterdam in
the distance and a cottage with trees and a
garden in the left foreground. c. 1655-6
With a collector's mark of a five-pointed star
blind-stamped in the top right-hand corner
(not recorded by Lugt).
Pen and ink and wash on brown paper.
7.8 x 21 cm.
Benesch links this *plein air* study to a small
group of similar landscapes executed in 'a kind
of shorthand or telegraphic style....evolved
from the geometrization of landscape'. In
them he considered that 'Rembrandt achieved
a particular vibrancy...which corresponds to
the vibrancy and sparkle of the brush-work in
his mature paintings'. It was largely as a result
of such work that the drawn sketch began to be
valued as an independent mode of expression.
Bibl: O. Benesch, *The Drawings of Rembrandt*,
1954-57, vol. 6, no. 1363.

68. Francesco Salviati (1510-1563); Italian
Portrait of a youth, head and shoulders,
full-face
Black chalk. 27 x 21.6 cm.
On the back of the mount is an inscription in
an eighteenth-century hand stating that the
drawing, like many others bought by the
writer, 'was in the Medici Collection in old
frames... thrown out as lumber'.
Bibl: Ward-Jackson I 280.

as Canaletto's vision of London's Montagu House perched on a Venetian canal (plate XV): scenes which, by evoking the spirit of a number of fashionable places, attached to the buyer a suggestion of *savoir-vivre*. More sophisticated was the demand for such visual puns as the *trompe-l'oeil* drawing reproduced as plate XII.

One measure of the growing popularity of drawings was the variety of print-making techniques that were perfected to imitate the specific qualities of different drawing media. Aquatint joined etching and printing from woodblocks as a method of imitating pen and wash drawings; the crayon method, a type of etching in which the marks through the ground are made with small toothed maces and roulettes, was developed to reproduce red and black chalk drawings. Such was the fashion for drawings by the end of the eighteenth century that artists such as Boucher and Greuze (plate XVI) were drawing scenes expressly for multiplication in one of these techniques, the prints themselves being collectors' items: as we have seen, many of Watteau's drawings were engraved after his death (Boucher was in fact among the artists employed to engrave some of them).

Another aspect of this enthusiasm was the increasing importance attached to drawing as a necessary accomplishment of the cultivated person. In 1661 Henry Peacham's *The Gentlemans Exercise of An exquisite practise, as well for drawing all manner of Beasts in their true Portraittures; as also the making of all kinds of colours, to be used in Lymning, Painting & C*, including lengthy passages on the tools and technique of drawing was re-published, together with *The Compleat Gentleman: Fashioning Him absolute in the most Necessary and Commendable Qualities concerning Mind or Body, that may be required in a Person of Honour*. Three years earlier, William Sanderson, after a quick history of art and some advice on where to hang paintings went on in *Graphice – The use of the Pen and Pencil, or, The Most Excellent Art Of Painting*: 'I have marvailed, at the negligence of parents in generall; they not to enforce a necessity, in the education of their

youth, to this art of drawing and designing, being so proper for any course of life whatsoever. Since the use thereof for expressing the conceptions of the mind, seems little inferiour, to that of writing; which in no man, ought to be deficient. And in many cases, drawing and designing performs, what by words are impossible; and (to boot) perfects the hand, for all manner of writing. And, if it be the generall rule, (or should be) that children be taught some gentel manufacture; then, doth this of drawing, apt them for those. For almost, nay in any art, we must respect rule, and proportion, which this makes perfect.'[21]

The reason for the special value many people attach to drawings was clearly expressed by Antoine Dézallier d'Argenville, himself an avid collector, in his *Abrégé de la vie des plus fameux peintres* published in 1762: 'The drawings of great masters, being all spirit, offer the most enthralling charm to the inquisitive; they are the best school for an art lover and a fertile source from which he may

70. Giovanni Benedetto Castiglione
(known as Il Grechetto) (c. 1610-1663 or
1665); Italian
Pan and Syrinx, with a river god
personifying the River Ladon, and two putti.
Mid-1650s
Red and brown oil paint, slightly coloured in
blue, green and violet, and heightened with
white. 41.2 x 42.4 cm.

Castiglione capitalised on the increasing
fashion for the sketch, producing rich, fluid
compositions illustrating popular themes
such as this one from Ovid's *Metamorphoses*
as a trademark of his studio. Executed in his
individual technique in which pigments in
linseed oil were brushed with a few fluent
strokes onto paper, it is superficially
reminiscent of the oil sketches on panel by
Rubens and Van Dyck. The composition is
based in reverse on a painting of the same
subject by Poussin of which three other
related drawings by Castiglione are known.
Bibl: Ward-Jackson II 668.

71. Antoine Watteau (1674-1721); French
Standing bearded oriental, wearing a fur hat
and leaning on a stick; and a separate
study of a hatless head.
Red chalk. 31.9 x 18 cm.

Watteau frequently drew scenic figures such
as this. Although it may have been made to
add to his repertoire of exotic figures for use
in a fête galante, it was not in fact used in
this way. The demand for such drawings as
collectors' pieces is proved by the existence
of a number in counterproof. None are
known of this drawing but there does exist
another version of the head on the right
which is almost exactly the same, in reverse.
After Watteau's death Jean de Jullienne
had over three hundred of his drawings
published in two volumes of *Figures de
différents Caractères, de Paysages et d'Etudes*,
1726 and 1728, and that version was
engraved by Laurent as number 16.
Bibl: K.T. Parker and J. Mathey, *Antoine
Watteau, catalogue complet de son oeuvre
dessiné*, 1957, no. 801.

72. Anonymous; Italian
Trompe l'oeil composition of engravings, drawings, a page from a calendar, a franked envelope and coins. Mid-eighteenth century
Pen and ink, wash and red chalk
21.3 x 29.6 cm. (detail)
This *trompe l'oeil* drawing shows the kind of technical virtuosity displayed by seventeenth and eighteenth century artists working in the strongly Baroque tradition of illusionism. The subject matter, with its superposition of different kinds of paper drawn over or printed in various media, is typical of its period, and also makes a kind of pun on the drawing itself. See Plate XII.

73. Antonio Canal (called Canaletto)
(1697-1768); Italian
Architectural *capriccio*, with
reminiscences of Montagu House, London
Pen and ink and wash over pencil
25.1 x 38.4 cm. (detail)
This drawing, probably made in Venice
after Canaletto's return there from London
in 1755, includes a number of architectural
motifs from the terrace of old Montagu
House beside the Thames. Existing features,
such as the cube-shaped pavilion over-
looking the water and the house with the
classical pediment on the right (albeit the
latter considerably altered in scale) are
combined with imaginary structures such as
the classical porch, to create a solely
decorative drawing of no topographical
import. Three or four similar drawings
incorporating echoes of Montagu Terrace
with the artist's own inventions are known.
Bibl: Ward-Jackson II 849. See Plate XV.

74. Jean-Auguste-Dominque Ingres
(1780-1867); French
Portrait of Mrs John Mackie
Signed *Ingres à Rome 1816*
Pencil. 17 x 16.5 cm.
Ingres' Roman portrait drawings were commissioned for their own sake, as souvenirs
for the sitters. The development of the
pencil, with its easily sharpened point,
coincided with a stylistic movement away
from the fluid blocks of tone of the Baroque
and Rococo, towards the style of clear
outline associated with Neo-Classicism.
This drawing demonstrates some of the
wide range of effects which can be obtained
with various hardnesses of pencil and
different movements and pressures of the
artist's hand.
Bibl: H. Naef, *Die Bildniszeichnungen von
J.-A.-D. Ingres*, 1977, IV, no. 169.

75. John Constable, RA (1776-1837); British
Stonehenge
Page from a sketch-book
Inscribed by the artist *15 July 1820* and on
the back *Stone Henge*
Pencil. 11.5 x 18.7 cm.
It was to this study, made during his only
recorded visit to Stonehenge, that Constable
turned fifteen years later, when the idea for
a large finished piece entered his mind. The
motif of the pensive figure who casts his
transient shadow on a stone is already
present. For the finished watercolour see
Plate XVII (a wash study, squared for
enlargement and transfer to the exhibition
drawing, is in the collection of the Victoria
and Albert Museum).
Bibl: G. Reynolds, *Catalogue of the Constable
Collection*, 1973, no. 186.

XVII. John Constable, RA (1776-1837); British
Stonehenge. 1835
Water-colour. 38.7 x 59.1 cm.
This water-colour was exhibited at the Royal Academy (no. 581) in 1836. It is laid down on what may be presumed to be the original mount, with a gilt line round the drawing. The mount bears the evocative inscription: 'The mysterious monument of Stonehenge, standing remote on a bare and boundless heath, as much unconnected with the events of the past ages as it is with the ones of the present, carries back beyond all historical records with the obscurity of a totally unknown period.'
Bibl: G. Reynolds, *Catalogue of the Constable Collection*, 1973, no. 395.

XVIII. Joseph Mallord William Turner
(1775-1851); British
Landscape, perhaps the Lake of Brienz
Water-colour. 37.5 x 54.5 cm.
Turner's late paintings are the finest expression of the atmospheric possibilities of pure
water-colour.
XIX. Paul Cézanne (1839-1906); French
Study of Trees (Sous Bois). *c.* 1887-89
Water-colour and pencil. 49.5 x 32 cm.
Cézanne tended to draw in pencil in order to commit moments to memory rather than to
make works as ends in themselves but, from the late 1880s, he became increasingly
interested in water-colours as a self-sufficient means of expression. However, his water-
colours are not coloured pencil drawings. His method of laying on spots of colour,
sometimes on top of one another (the spots being left to dry between the application of each
layer to stop them running together) enabled him to suggest line and form through colour
by less cumbersome means than oil paint: a simple technique was especially important to
him as he painted many of his subjects in the open air.
Bibl: L. Venturi. *Cézanne son art, son œuvre*, 1936, no. 1621.

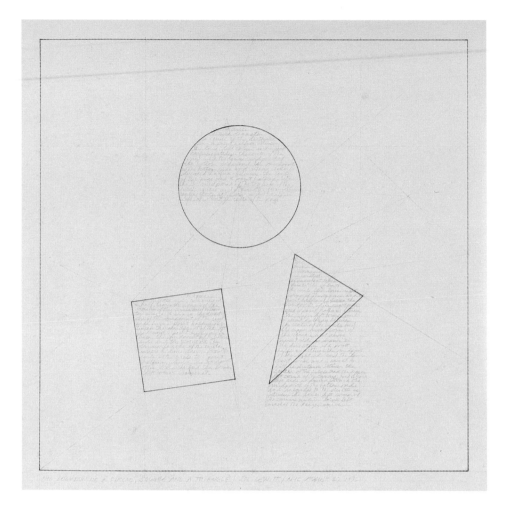

THE LOCATION OF A CIRCLE, SQUARE AND A TRIANGLE / SOL LEWITT / NYC AUGUST 20 1975

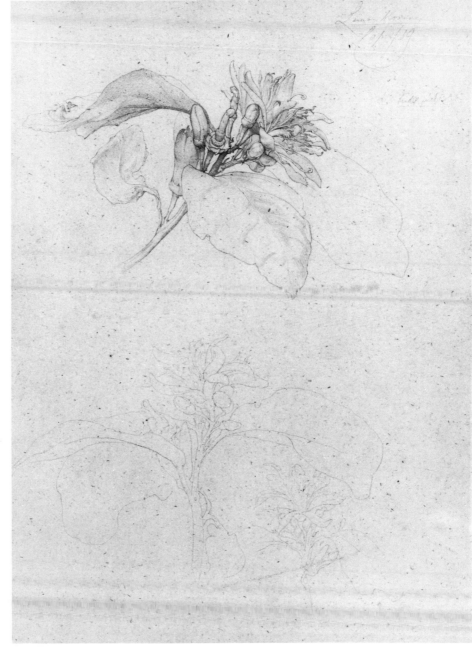

76. Frederic Leighton (Baron Leighton of Stretton) (1830-1896); British
Three studies, one shaded and two in outline, of lemon blossom. 1859
Inscribed *Lemon blossom. Capri/59* and *buds pink violet*
Pencil on toned paper. 22.8 x 15.7 cm.
Mrs Russell Barrington records that Leighton showed her this drawing with 'words to the effect that it was not only the Pre-Raphaelites who reverenced the detail in Nature, and who thought it worth the time and labour it took to record the beauty in the wonderful minutiae of her structure'. This is an on-the-spot study of the kind of blossom that appears again and again in his paintings.
Bibl: Mrs Russell Barrington, *The Life, Letters and Works of Frederic Leighton*, 1906, I, p. 202.

XX Sol LeWitt. *See* fig. 80.

78. Henri de Toulouse-Lautrec (1864-1901);
French
Study related to the poster the 'Troupe de
Mlle Eglantine', 1896
Pencil 11 6 x 18,5 cm.
A sketch quickly drawn at the cabaret and
later adapted for a poster design.

77. Paul Gauguin (1848-1903); French
Head of a Tahitian man. 1891-93
Oiled charcoal on buff paper. 39.5 x 31 cm.
While in Tahiti Gauguin made a considerable number of drawings, some of which he
later assembled in a personal portfolio
entitled *Documents - Tahiti, 1891, 1892,
1893*. These he was to use as a source for
details in his paintings in the following
years. His belief in the essentially private
nature of drawing was expressed in *Avant et
après*: 'A critic at my house sees some
paintings. Greatly perturbed he asks for my
drawings. My drawings? Never! They are
my letters, my secrets.'
Bibl: R. Pickvance, *The drawings of Gaugin*,
1970, p. 5.

draw all the illumination he can need; he will talk, so to speak, he will hobnob
with and learn from these celebrities; looking over a collection of their drawings
he will become their familiar.'[22] For as the historian, Woldemar von Seidlitz
pointed out in *Leonardo da Vinci, der Wendepunkt der Renaissance* (1909)
'drawings should not ... be considered as results of a special sort of artistic
activity, separated from works in sculpture, architecture, or painting but rather
as objects intimately connected with executed works, because they often
witness to parts of the whole creative process which can seldom or never be
satisfactorily externalized in other ways; above all drawings, more immediately
than "published" works, give an insight into the spiritual life of the artist, and
hence are weighty documents for the study and understanding of his
activity.'[23]

Stemming from the artist's use of drawing as a means of visualising thought
came the feeling that drawings were intimate works which brought one close to
the artist's process of creation. Capitalising on this idea some artists, including
the Carracci, made drawings for sale which looked like sketches for more
ambitious work. The drawing by Castiglione in figure 70 is an example of this,
though in fact the vigorous pursuit of Syrinx by Pan is derived from a painting
by Poussin.

Certain drawings, such as pastel compositions, some kinds of water-colours
(especially in England, for example exhibition pieces by Constable (plate XVII)
and Turner (plate XVIII)) and some portrait drawings, have always taken their
place beside paintings but until this century the majority of drawings have been
small in scale and relatively private in intention. It is only comparatively
recently that drawings conceived as finished works have taken on the breadth
of subject and the public appearance of works on canvas. International
exhibitions of contemporary drawings as distinct from painting shows are

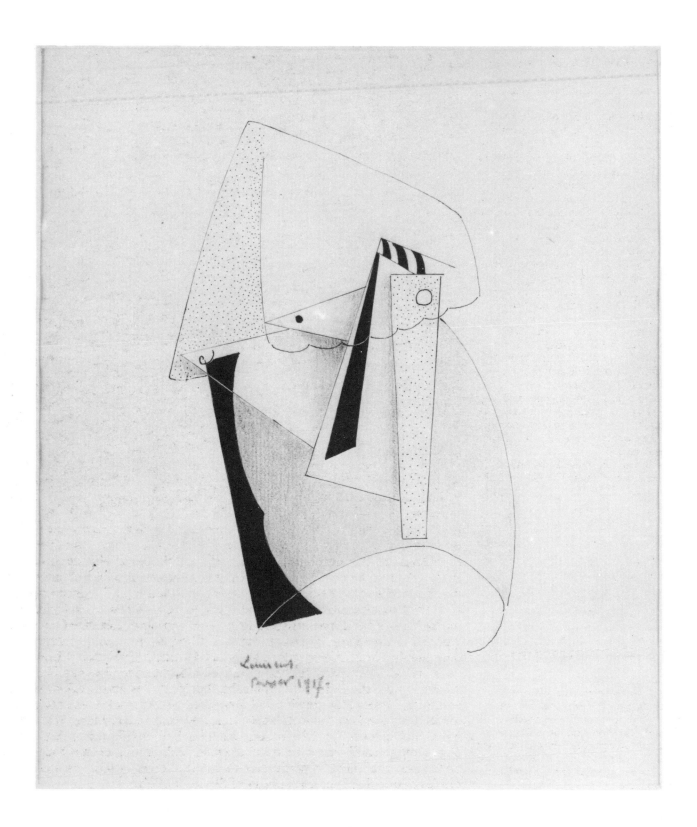

80. Sol LeWitt (born 1928); USA
The location of a circle, square and a triangle
Signed and dated *Sol LeWitt/NYC August 27 1976.*
Inscribed with a description of the plan.
Pencil and pen and ink on tracing paper
48 x 48 cm.
This drawing is one result of Sol LeWitt's research into lines and geometric structures. Though it is a work in its own right, not a preliminary study, it is the idea behind it rather than its realization that is important. Of conceptual art, the artist has written: 'the idea or concept is the most important aspect of the work. When an artist uses a conceptual form of art, it means that all of the planning and decisions are made beforehand and the execution is a perfunctory affair. The idea becomes a machine that makes the art. This kind of art is not theoretical or illustrative of theories: it is intuitive, it is involved with all types of mental processes and it is purposeless. It is usually free from the dependence of the skill of the artist as a craftsman. It is the objective of the artist who is concerned with conceptual art to make his work mentally interesting to the spectator, and therefore usually he would want it to become emotionally dry.'
Bibl: *Sol LeWitt*, catalogue for an exhibition at the Gemeentemuseum, The Hague, 1970, p. 56.

79. Henri Laurens (1885-1954); French
Tête
Signed and dated *1917*
Pencil and ink and pencil. 30 x 23 cm.
Between 1916 and 1918, Laurens made a number of polychromed constructions in wood, card and sheet-iron, of heads, figures and still-life subjects. This finished drawing is closely related to but independent of these works. In it, different materials are indicated by dots, shading and opaque black.

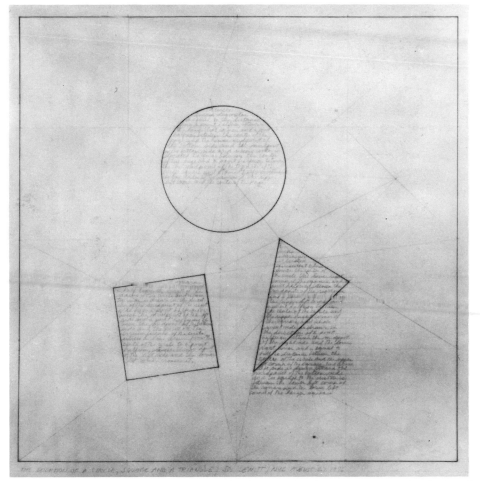

becoming regular events. This is partly the result of an increase in the scale of paper easily available: only since the nineteenth century has paper been manufactured in dimensions larger than those of the old handmade sheets. But there are not just mechanical explanations for the increase of interest in drawings: it is more to do with the artist's self-awareness, his preoccupation with the artistic process and the resulting value attached to exploring each medium to its full. Some artists followed the example of Cézanne (plate XIX) who did not recognise the existence of drawing as an activity separate from painting. In a letter to Emile Bernard he said 'while one paints, one draws; the more the colour harmonizes, the more precise becomes the drawing. When the colour is rich, the form is at its height. The contrasts and relations of tone comprise the secret of drawing and form' for 'the form and contour of objects are conveyed to us through opposition and contrast resulting from their individual colours'[24], while others, such as Sol LeWitt (plate XX), have abstracted the different elements of drawing, and, putting them through both systematic and random permutations, made the characteristics and possibilities of drawing itself the subject of the work of art.

DRAWING FOR UTILITY

Facing page: Detail of Plate XXV. Sir John
Soane (1753-1837); British
Elevation of the façade and plan of the
portico of the Temple of Clitumnus, near
Spoleto, c. 1780
Inscribed *Il Tempietto De Clitumno and La
Pianta Del Portico*
Pen and ink and grey brown wash
37.6 x 40.8 cm.
Soane journeyed in Italy from 1778 to 1780,
having been sent there by the Royal
Academy as a Travelling Student in order to
complete his architectural studies. Professor
Du Prey quotes a letter to Soane from Lady
Anne Riggs Miller (author of *Letters from
Italy ... By an Englishwoman*, 1776), dated
25 June 1780, and replying with thanks 'for
all your kind attentions to me and in
particular for the sketch of the Temple of
Clitumnus which I am quite impatient to
possess ...' Du Prey concludes that Soane
had sketched the little temple probably in
the hope that a presentation drawing would
induce Lady Miller to commission a similar
building for her own garden. In this,
however, he was disappointed. The drawing
exhibited here is a copy retained by Soane.
Bibl: Pierre de la Ruffinière Du Prey, *John
Soane's architectural education 1753-80*, 1977,
p. 241.

None of the drawings in this chapter was produced for the sake of the image itself only: all were made for an ulterior reason and some of them have no artistic aspirations at all. This category includes presentation drawings made to obtain commissions or done to assist the client's imagination, drawings done as instructions to craftsmen and technicians responsible for producing finished works, diagrams and technical illustrations, and drawings done to provide patterns or to keep a visual record.

Most of the drawings have been made after the creative thinking has been completed, and they have further in common the effect their ulterior purpose has on their style. For example, presentation drawings, whether for a competition or for the client, tend to have an alluring finish of either confidence-inspiring technical brilliance, as in James Paine's proposal for Wardour Castle (plate XXI), or of suggestive sketchiness: Raymond McGrath's atmospheric interior of Fischer's restaurant (plate XXII) being a case in point. Drawings made for execution in other techniques are influenced by the appearance and possibilities of their intended media. For instance, a drawing made for reproduction as a wood-engraving, such as Millais' Cleopatra in figure 87, will tend to imitate the linear quality of the finished product so that the latter can be true to the original. Working drawings for woven textiles (figs. 84 & 85) may distinguish the different sorts of strokes. Diagrammatic drawings and technical illustrations rely on simplification according to certain conventions for their clarity: a classic example is the design by Beck for the London Underground map (fig. 91), which has had a major effect on designers. The tendency to simplify is visible in many drawings executed as patterns, being a characteristic which allows for them to be followed by each artist in his own medium and style: the drawing by Chippendale in figure 93 was for his own very successful and influential pattern book, the *Gentleman and Cabinet-Maker's Director*. Record drawings combine simplification with detailed treatment in order to make the record as clear as possible: the sheet of designs of stage properties in figure 96 expressly shows the form and colouring of the props rather than their setting or use.

The subject of drawing for utility is a vast one, which many artists of importance, including, from the selection here Aubrey Beardsley (fig. 88), Georges Braque (fig. 89) and Emil Nolde (fig. 98) have contributed. But a connoisseurly approach to drawing has tended to lead such drawings to be

81. John Michael Rysbrack (1694-1770);
British
Design for a monument to General Wolfe.
c. 1760
Inscribed with scale and inscribed on the
back in ink with a description of the
monument and *The Height 19 feet 1 inch.
Width 11 feet 11 inches* and in pencil
M. Rysbrack delt. Inscribed in ink with the
mark of the collection of Charles Rogers
(Lugt 624)
Pen and ink, water-colour and ink wash
33.5 x 24.3 cm.
Wolfe is represented dying and supported
by the Goddess of War, with Britannia
lamenting over him and Fame descending
to crown him. On the pedestal is a relief
depicting Wolfe being carried dead into the
city of Quebec.

After Parliament had resolved to erect a
monument to Wolfe in Westminster Abbey
in London, designs were submitted by
several artists, including J.F. Roubiliac,
Robert Adam, William Chambers, Henry
Cheere, William Tyler and Joseph Wilton,
as well as Rysbrack. (Wilton's design was
chosen and the monument unveiled in
1773.)

The clear outline of this drawing, and the
use of colour to indicate the materials
intended in the monument, suggest that it
was made for presentation to the selecting
committee rather than for the artist's own
use. It was once in the possession of
Charles Rogers, the collector and print
publisher, who probably obtained it as part
of his purchases from Rysbrack in 1765 and
1766. A reversed version of the design, with
some changes of detail and before the
addition of the bas-relief on the base, is also
in the collection of the Victoria and Albert
Museum.

XXI. James Paine (c. 1716-1789), British

Wardour Castle, Wiltshire. Section through the centre of the house from north to south showing the entrance hall, circular staircase, upper landing and coffered dome supported on Corinthian columns. c. 1768

Inscribed with scale.

Pen and ink and water-colour. 59.7 x 47.9 cm.

Paine was commissioned by Henry, 8th Lord Arundell of Wardour, to design a new and imposing mansion in the grounds of Wardour Park, so that the family could re-establish itself there, on the site of the ancestral domain, in a manner befitting its recently acquired wealth. Building was begun in 1768 and completed in 1776.

This is a finished drawing, one of many which the architect would have prepared for Lord Arundell in order to show him his proposed plans clearly and attractively. A section of the house from south to north is reproduced in *Plans, Elevations, and Sections of Noblemen and Gentlemen's Houses ...* by James Paine, vol. 2, published in London, 1783.

XXII. Raymond B. McGrath (1903-1977); Australian, worked in Britain
Design for Fischer's Restaurant and Long Bar, New Bond Street, London.
Perspective view of the cashier's desk and cloaks counter. 1932
Pencil, colour crayon and gouache on tracing paper. 27 x 33.5 cm.
The drawing emphasizes the room's curvilinear character. The sweep of the staircase with its chrome handrails curving round the cashier's desk, is played off against the outer curve of the internally-lit, lowered ceiling, and the striking coral-red column provides a pivot for the whole space. It is one of several studies which the architect made to convey to the client, in an atmospheric way, the structure, colour and lighting of his interiors for Fischer's Restaurant.

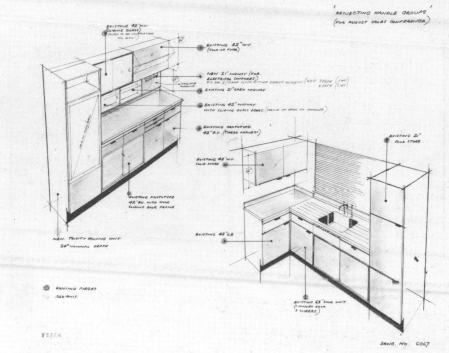

82. George Fejér (born 1912); British
'Projecting Handle Groups'
Drawing showing arrangements of a range
of kitchen units and fittings designed by
George Fejér for Hygena Ltd. 1962
Inscribed with title, *(For August Sales
Conference)* and with notes pin-pointing
existing and additional items in the range.
Numbered *Drwg. No. 6067* and stamped
Fejér
Pen and ink and coloured crayons
Size of sheet 40.6 x 50.5 cm.
As the inscriptions make clear, this drawing
was made for a forthcoming sales conference
at which the designer was to show his latest
additions to a range of Hygena kitchen
units. It was necessary that the contents of
the drawing should be quickly understood,
and to this end it is attractively presented
and clearly labelled.

appreciated for their aesthetic qualities alone, with the original reason for their
existence, and therefore an important contributory factor to their appearance,
being forgotten. Here drawings by distinguished artists are discussed in the
context of their function, alongside the more mundane drawings of lesser
names and the somewhat anonymous products of drawing offices. The types of
drawing discussed only suggest some among many of the utilitarian ends which
drawing may serve.

PRESENTATION DRAWINGS

Since the introduction of paper to the West drawings have been used as a means
of explaining what a completed work in other media (and often in three
dimensions) will look like, and such drawings have often been made in order to
obtain a commission either privately or through a competition. Such drawings
for paintings are sometimes referred to by the Italian word *modelli*. As the
purpose of these drawings is to impress a prospective patron they are often
more finished than the sketches made by the artist for his own use during the
creation of the design, and have the materials of the intended product
attractively suggested, as with Rysbrack's design for a monument (fig. 81).
Similar drawings have been and still are used to help a client envisage what a
proposed design will look like or to enable the designer to discuss alternatives
with him. George Fejér's drawing of kitchen units (fig. 82) is a modern
example.

83. Battista Franco (known as Semolei)
(c. 1498-1561); Italian
Design for a majolica dish
A scene from classical history or mythology,
with a young soldier on his knees kissing the
hands of an old man; the border decorated
with putti
With the mark of the collection of Sir J.
Richardson (Lugt 2184)
Pen and ink and wash. Diameter 26 cm.
According to Vasari, Franco made many
designs for the Duke of Urbino's majolica
factory at Castel Durante, including several
for a service presented to Charles V and
another given to Cardinal Farnese, brother-
in-law of Duke Guidobaldo II. Clifford and
Mallet have partially reconstructed, from
drawings and surviving pieces of majolica, a
'History of Troy' service with which this
drawing is probably connected. They
identify the old man as King Priam and the
kneeling warrior as Hector taking leave
before fighting Achilles, or Paris asking
permission to marry Helen.

All the known drawings relating to this
service have concentric circles, drawn with a
compass and, usually, two circumferences
incised with a stylus. Invariably the border
designs are worked up on one side only,
indicating to the majolica painter to provide
a mirror image on the other side. No dish
bearing the central composition of this
design has been found, but one bearing the
same arrangement of putti around the rim is
known. Presumably this area of the design
was indented with a stylus in order to
transfer it to another surface.
Bibl: T. Clifford and J.V.G. Mallet, 'Battista
Franco as a designer for Majolica', *The
Burlington Magazine*, 118, 1976, p. 404.
Ward-Jackson I 141.

Sometimes these drawings are made by the designer himself but they may be
produced equally by a lesser hand from his studio or by an artist specifically
employed to put the ideas on paper in an attractive way: this is particularly true
of architectural perspective drawings.

DRAWINGS FOR PRODUCTION IN OTHER MEDIA

The form of these drawings varies enormously according to the conventions of
the finished medium, certain colours, sorts of line and so forth giving specific
information or demanding certain actions from craftsmen in a particular field.
Such conventions are often non-naturalistic: that is, they stand for or
symbolise things without imitating or seeking to represent them directly. Some
of the drawings are referred to by specialist terms. For example a cartoon is a
full-sized drawing made with the intention of transferring its design, by
pricking, pouncing or some other method, to a surface such as a wall, for a
mural, canvas, for a painting, glass as in figure 86, preparatory to cutting and
staining, or tapestry. The squared drawings of the textile technician, like figure

84. Anna Maria Garthwaite (1690-1763);
British
Design for a Spitalfield woven silk. 1747
Inscribed on the backing paper *Mr Vautier
July 9 1747* and *306 Cords 8 & 8.* Numbered
17
Pen and purple ink and wash, squared in
pencil for transfer. 32.4 x 17.1 cm.

The drawing is the artist's original design
which would later have been squared up by
a draughtsman into a working drawing. The
spotting on the design indicates that it is for
a tabby, or plain weave, which has a slightly
granular texture. The purple ink and wash
denote that the pattern is of one colour, and
the wash areas tell the weaver that extra
threads are to be floated over the weft to
create the flowers, leaves, etc. Probably the
background pattern is formed by an inter-
ruption of the ground weave. The design
would have been woven on a draw-loom,
and the '306 cords' in the inscription denote
the number of warp-carrying cords which
will pass over the pulley of the loom and
which, when raised by a draw boy, will
allow the insertion of weft threads by the
weaver.

'Mr Vautier' in the inscription is probably
Daniel Vautier (*c.* 1694-1760?), a master
weaver who was one of Anna Maria Garthwaite's most important customers.

85. Anonymous; British
Detail from a point paper of floral design, for a Jacquard-woven textile produced by Arthur H. Lee & Sons Ltd, 1899.
Dated in ink on the back *July 1899* and inscribed in ink *Design 115* and with the number of weft lines (1 to 657) in the repeat of the design and number of dents (3 to 50) (the number of spaces between the vertical bars of the reed through which the warp ends are drawn) in the reed. Inscribed again on the back with instructions for cutting the Jacquard cards. With stamp of paper manufacturers Howitt & Son, Nottingham Water- and body-colour on 6 x 9 point paper. Size of sheet 78 x 51.7 cm.
This working drawing was made to scale by a professional draughtsman from the original artist's design. It gives information to the weaver for setting up the pattern to the loom; each square of the point-paper contains six vertical lines corresponding to the warp and nine horizontal lines corresponding to the weft, signifying that the warp thread will be slightly thicker than the weft. It also gives instructions about the cutting of the cards for the Jacquard loom on which the design is to be woven: each painted rectangle within the squares denotes the appearance in the weft line of the appropriately coloured thread, and thus is a precise guide to the holes which are to be punched in the cards to allow this thread to be raised in weaving. See plate XXIII.

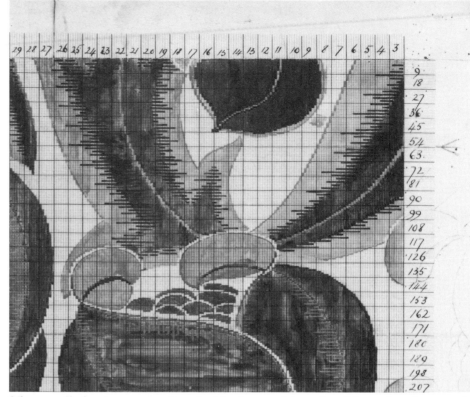

85, are called point papers. Inevitably the graphic style of these drawings tends to be influenced by the intended medium. This is particularly the case in drawings for book illustration as can be seen by comparing Millais' drawing for wood-engraving (fig. 87) and Beardsley's for photogravure (fig. 88). Their style is influenced also by their role in the production process. For example, the products of drawing offices, like the drawings of a carving fork in figure 90 have the same simple clarity as the technical illustrations discussed below for both are intended to be understood by third parties (fig. v and 92).

Some of these drawings do show how the design has been arrived at. This is common in Renaissance examples when the artist and the craftsman were often the same person, and remains true where the relationship is close, like that of a dress designer and his cutter: it is the case with Braque's work for the Ballets Russes (fig. 89). But many production drawings, especially those connected with architecture and modern technology, are made by professional draughtsmen following instructions rather than by designers. The carving fork already mentioned was designed by Robert Welch but the drawings were made by someone trained specifically to make drawings for factory production. The organisation of drawing offices developed enormously during the nineteenth century. By taking design away from the craftsman and allowing management to exercise more precise control, drawing offices played a significant part in the mechanization of production and thus in the emergence of the fully industrialized Western society.

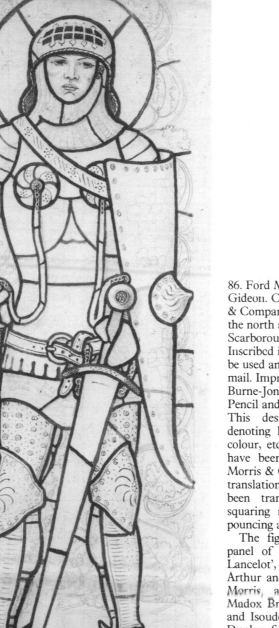

86. Ford Madox Brown (1821-1893); British
Gideon. Cartoon commissioned by Morris
& Company for a stained glass window in
the north aisle of St Martin's-on-the-Hill,
Scarborough. 1862
Inscribed in pencil with notes on colours to
be used and areas to be painted with chain-
mail. Impressed with stamp of Sir Edward
Burne-Jones, Bart.
Pencil and wash; squared. 99.4 x 36.2 cm.
This design, with its main wash-line
denoting lead lines and with its notes on
colour, etc., is a final cartoon which would
have been passed to a craftsman at the
Morris & Company glass-painting studio for
translation into the medium of glass. It has
been transferred to this sheet by the
squaring method: there are also signs of
pouncing and of work with a stylus.

The figure depicted also appears in a
panel of stained glass 'King Arthur and
Lancelot', in which the figure of King
Arthur and the background are by William
Morris, and the figure of Lancelot by
Madox Brown. This, part of the 'Tristram
and Isoude' series commissioned by Walter
Dunlop for Harden Grange, Yorkshire, in
1862, is now in Bradford City Art Gallery.
A cartoon for the whole design is in the
William Morris Gallery, Walthamstow
(no. A.262).
Bibl: A Charles Sewter, *The Stained Glass of
William Morris and His Circle*, New Haven
and London, 1974, p. 69.

87. Sir John Everett Millais (1829-1896); British

Cleopatra. Drawing for a wood-engraved illustration to 'A Dream of Fair Women' by Alfred, Lord Tennyson, published in Moxon's *Tennyson*, 1857, reproduced with a proof of the wood-engraving by W.J. Linton Brush and ink. 9.5 x 8.3 cm.; wood-engraving. 9.7 x 8.3 cm.

Until the mid-nineteenth century drawings for wood-engravings were made on the block and so lost in the cutting process. In this drawing Millais benefited from the recent development of photographic processes which could transfer an original image to a printing block. He worked directly on paper, and made his drawing the same way round as he wished it to be printed, leaving the camera to reverse it in the transfer process. Some illustrations also used the photographic process to enlarge or reduce the drawn image. The fine lines drawn with a brush, some of them delineating positive uninked areas as in the grass behind the figure, actually imitate both the black and the white lines produced by the medium by which they were to be reproduced.

88. Aubrey Beardsley (1872-1898); British
How King Arthur saw the Questing Beast
and thereof had a great marvel
Drawing for a photogravure frontispiece to
Vol.I of Sir Thomas Malory's *Le Morte
Darthur*, published by J.M. Dent & Co,
London, 1893-4
Signed within the design *Aubrey Beardsley*
and with the artist's emblem, and dated
March 8 1893
Pen and ink and wash. 37.8 x 27.1 cm.
This is an elaborate composition very finely
drawn, and, as Brian Reade notes, 'there is a
strange profusion of what amounts almost to
automatic drawing in the details that
decorate every part of the landscape: these
include a treble clef, a signature, a spider's
web, a phallus and calligraphic flourishes in
the manner of the seventeenth-century
writing masters.'

Beardsley was one of the first artists to
make drawings specifically for reproduction
by photo-mechanical processes. He realized
that the printing process could enhance the
quality of the drawing, the velvety tones of
photogravure, for example, bringing out the
best qualities in his wash drawings, like this
one, and the sharpness of line-block giving
precision to his line drawings.
Bibl: B.Reade, *Beardsley*, 1967 no. 56.

89. Georges Braque (1882-1963); French
Design for the costume of a Valet, in
Molière's one-act comedy-ballet *Les Fâcheux*
with music by Georges Auric, first produced
by the Ballet Russes in Monte Carlo,
19 January 1924
Inscribed with directions to the costumier
Pencil and body-colour. 31 x 23.3 cm.
Les Fâcheux was Braque's first experiment
with theatrical design, although his repu-
tation in the field of fine art was already
established. He discussed his designs with
Diaghilev in the autumn of 1923, and
produced a series of freely-drawn, imaginative sketches which gave a general
impression of the Louis XIV costumes, but
left most of the technical manufacturing
details to be worked out by the costumier.
Bibl: J. Cocteau, *Les Fâcheux*, 1924;
H. Rischbieter, *Art and the stage in the 20th
century*, 1969, pp. 84, 89, 268-9.

XXIII. Anonymous. *See* fig. 85.

Design 115

39

A.M.3267ᵃ.-'56.   V. A. M.

XXIV Jacques le Moyne. *See* fig. 92.

·IL·TEMPIETTO·DI·CLITVMNO·

·LA·PIANTA· ·DEL·PORTICO·

XXV. Sir John Soane (1753-1837); British
Elevation of the façade and plan of the portico of the Temple of Clitumnus, near Spoleto.

XXVI Anonymous. *See* fig. 85.

90. Robert Welch (born 1929)/ Robert
Welch Associates; British
Three working drawings for the 'Alveston'
stainless-steel carving fork for Old Hall
Tableware Ltd. 1964
a. Body dimensions. Plan and section to full-
size scale.
Dated *20 Jan 64*. Inscribed *drn: N.M.* and
with job and drawing description.
Numbered *RW 249/2/1*
Pen and indian ink on tracing paper.
35.1 x 47.3 cm.
b. Guard movement. Section, drawn to scale
10 x full size.
Dated *20 Jan 64*. Inscribed *drn: N.M.* and
with job and drawing description.
Numbered *RW 249/1/2*
Pen and indian ink on tracing paper.
35.1 x 47.4 cm.
c. Guard fitting details. Dated *4 May 64*.
Inscribed *Drawn N.M.* and with job and
drawing descriptions.
Numbered *RW 259/1/3*
Pen and indian ink with some felt-tip on
tracing paper. 34.9 x 47.8 cm.

These drawings, made by a draughtsman in
the Robert Welch workshop, are part of a
series of precise construction guides to the
manufacture of the final handmade prototypes from which the dies of the 'Alveston'
carving set were cut. They represent an
advanced stage in the design process, having
been developed from Robert Welch's
original sketches and preliminary hand-
forged prototypes on which user tests had
been carried out. Drawing a. shows the
overall dimensions of the fork; drawing b.
shows the spring mechanism by which the
guard of the fork can be pushed to stand out
from it, and returned to lie flat along the
back of the fork; drawing c. clarifies
construction details.

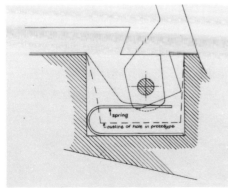

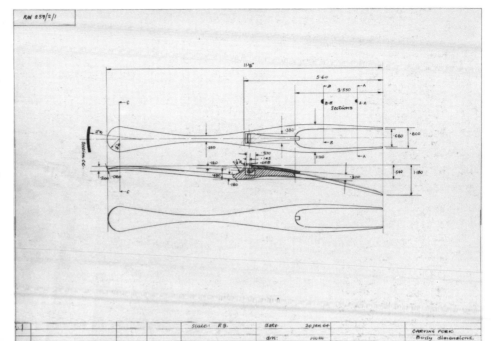

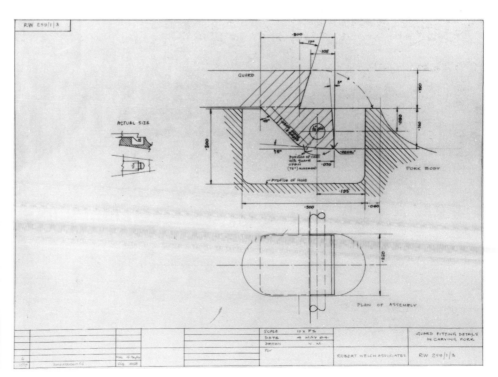

DIAGRAMS AND TECHNICAL ILLUSTRATIONS

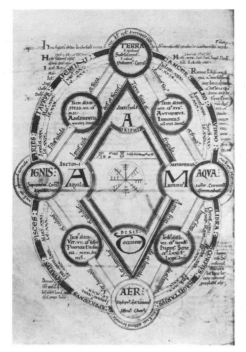

(iii) Ramsey Abbey, *c.* 1080-90
Natural science and computistical text-book
Cosmological diagram
Pen and ink and body colour on vellum
34.2 x 24.2 cm.
This diagram is one of several illustrating a selection of texts by Isidore of Seville, Bede and Abbo of Fleury put together in the early 11th century by Byrhtferth of Ramsey for the purpose of monastic teaching. It enumerates and correlates the Zodiac, the Months, the Seasons, the Elements, the four Ages of Man, the Cardinal Points and the Winds. Such diagrams, typical of medieval learning, not only illustrate the text but often go beyond it to convey fundamental themes of Christian cosmological doctrine.
C.M. Kauffmann, *Romanesque Manuscripts 1066-1190*, 1975, no. 9; *Manuscripts at Oxford: R.W. Hunt Memorial Exhibition*, Bodleian Library, 1980, IV.5.

Diagrams and technical illustrations use the simplification of line to describe something, to analyse the structure of an object or to express sets of relationships or chains of ideas or actions, without actually representing them, in a way which can be understood with greater speed than is possible through words. Both diagrams and technical illustrations are usually accompanied by explanatory text, even if only in the abbreviated form of a key.

Diagrams in some form or other are as old as civilisation and have been used frequently in the West since paper became available. During this time the concept of the diagram has not changed. The more or less decorated schematic tree has been used for centuries as a means of explaining any system of classification involving divisons and subdivisions. A contemporary flow-chart describing, for example, the movement of goods, whose responsibility they are and the time schedule which is to be worked to simultaneously is more complicated than a mediaeval astrological diagram (fig. iii) (the former attempts to express a moving continuity and the latter shows relationships at a particular moment) but they are not significantly different. Nevertheless the sign language has been developed and standardized by the introduction of more precise formulae. For example, the graph is a diagram that expresses with beautiful simplicity the successive changes in variable quantities. It was invented in the nineteenth century and was first used to advance thought in the field of chemistry but has since become one of the most widely used means of making the significance of measurement visible at a glance. The isotype chart, developed in Germany in the 1930s, using repeated symbols to portray relative amounts has brought complicated ideas concerning subjects such as economics within the grasp of the ordinary newspaper reader (fig. iv).

Technical illustrations are among the earliest surviving drawings (fig. v). A de-personalised drawing style has always been an important tool in man's desire to describe and quantify and thus understand the world in which he lives. Nowadays technical illustration is used when the power of drawing to express something more clearly and to direct the attention more concentratedly than is possible with illustrative photographs is required in, for example, instruction manuals (fig. 92).

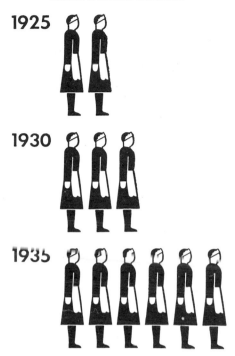

1925

1930

1935

(iv) Isotype Group; Austrian
Isotype chart. 1936
Lithograph. 11.5 x 6.5 cm.
This simple illustration appeared in Otto
Neurath's *International Picture Language* in
which the theory behind Isotype (International
System of Typographic Picture Education), a
system for the presentation of information
by the repetition of drawn symbols, was
explained. Like all modern diagrams
intended for the general public, the finished
form of the isotype is printed. This visual
approach to the presentation of calculations
has greatly influenced graphic design.

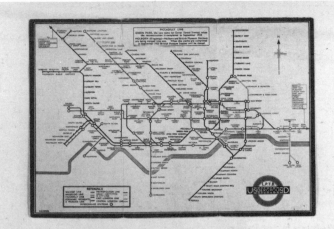

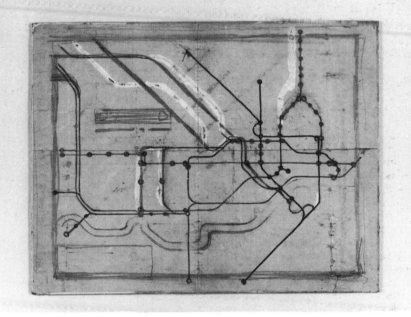

91. Henry C. Beck (1901-1974); British
Design for the London Underground
Railway map, with a copy of the map. 1931
Pencil and coloured inks on squared paper
pasted onto card. Size of sheet 19 x 24 cm.
The diagrammatic map, which also enlarged
and clarified the central area, is much easier
to read than the geographically accurate
map in use from 1919 which it superseded
in the summer of 1933. Although the map
has undergone many modifications, it has
remained essentially the same design from
its inception to the present day and has been
one of the strongest influences on the
development of map and network design
this century.

92. Advisory Committee on Utility Furniture; British
Two drawings intended for publication in a *General Specification for Utility Furniture*, issued by the Board of Trade, 1942
Both pen and indian ink. 38.1 x 22.8 cm.
a. Component drawing for a chair or settee employing woven fibre.
Lettered with title, references to types of furniture to which this drawing was applicable, and numbered key of components. Numbered *Fig.15* and (page number) *43*
b. Constructional diagrams (2 on 1 sheet) for a mortise and tenon joint for door ends and top framing, and for methods of jointing table legs to frame rails.
Lettered with titles, references to types of furniture to which these drawings were applicable and with alternative dimensions of mortise and tenon joints. Numbered *Fig. 11* and *Fig. 12* and (page number) *39*. The Utility Furniture scheme was set up by the Board of Trade in 1942, and was organised by an advisory committee which worked throughout the war 'to produce specifications for furniture of good sound construction in simple but agreeable designs for sale at reasonable prices, and ensuring the maximum economy of raw materials and labour'. These specification drawings aimed to give designated manufacturers of the strictly rationed wartime furniture a precise guide to the materials and construction methods to be used in its production, as clearly and simply as possible.

(v) (?) English, Early 12th century
Medical tracts
Surgeon heating cautery irons; two naked male cautery figures
Pen and ink on vellum. 18.4 x 12.7 cm.
Cautery, a medical treatment consisting of the searing of designated spots with a hot iron was, together with blood-letting, one of the principal curatives of the Middle Ages. It was used to heal far more than external wounds. These two 'technical' illustrations show the irons being heated and the places of the body to which they should be applied. The simplified presentation, with no extraneous detail, makes them as easy to understand as, for example, illustrations in a modern first-aid manual.
C.M. Kauffmann, *Romanesque Manuscripts 1066-1190*, 1975, no. 12.

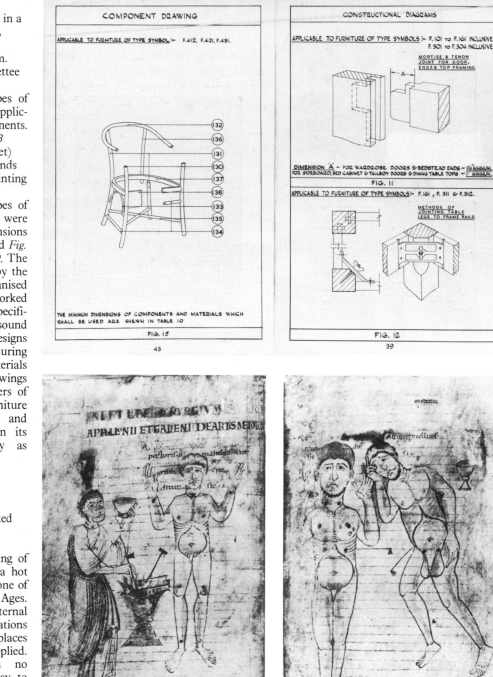

RECORD AND PATTERN DRAWINGS

Before the invention of photography drawing was the only means available of making simple two-dimensional records. It has been used to record all kinds of information, be it botanical, zoological, anatomical, medical or archaeological: an example of the latter is the tile in figure 97. Draughtsmen usually accompanied explorers in order to enable them to bring back a record of the appearance of the inhabitants, the land formation and the flora and fauna of unfamiliar countries, as in Nolde's drawing from German New Guinea in figure 98 or Le Moyne's, made after an expedition from France to Florida (plate XXIV). Such drawings have the advantage over photography that they can remove the desired information effortlessly from its irrelevant context and concentrate the attention on the subject that is being examined. Many such drawings are lifeless but others, of which Leonardo's anatomical studies must be the most famous, look so closely at whatever is being studied, and portray the essence of the subject with such power and sympathy that they have a value beyond that of the facts that they record.

Artists also use drawing to record technical details – the look of a specific piece of armour for use in some composition, or to record the appearance of a work that has been despatched to its new owner: Sir John Soane's drawing (plate XXV) is an example. Such records of paintings are sometimes referred to as *ricordi*. Similarly, factories often record their manufactures by simple line representation, recognising that both shapes and decoration can often be more quickly identified by such simplified drawings than by tonal photographs, especially where the same shape be used with a number of different designs in figure 95.

These record drawings have often been used by later generations as patterns to follow. Originality in composition has only been identified with innovation relatively recently. The painters of Byzantine icons, for example, aimed to follow the canonical pattern as faithfully as possible. Since then artists have collected the works of others in order to provide themselves with patterns and made drawings precisely to act as patterns for later artists and craftsmen. During the Middle Ages and the Renaissance these patterns were handed on from teacher to pupil, the latter sometimes making his own copy by one of the transfer methods. During the fifteenth century the first individual sheets and then books of patterns began to be printed. Gradually with the rise in status of the artist and craftsman and the introduction of copyright and patent laws, more emphasis was given to innovatory design. Nevertheless pattern books remained part of the craftsman's studio equipment well into this century and the designs of others are still one of the artist's most fruitful sources of inspiration.

XXIV. Jacques Le Moyne De Morgues (*c.* 1533-1588); French, worked in Britain from *c.* 1580
Lemon and Seville orange fruits (*citrus limon* and *citrus aurantium*)
On the back, a mulberry (*morus nigra*).
Numbered in ink *39*
Water- and body-colour. 22.2 x 16.8 cm.
The drawing is one of a series of 57 fruit and flower drawings by Le Moyne, which were identified in 1922 and extracted from an album which had been bought by the Museum Library in 1856 for the importance of its sixteenth century French binding. The evidence on other sheets of the watermark (found on paper in use in France between 1556 and 1568) and of titles inscribed in French as well as Latin, possibly by the artist, could suggest that the drawings were made before Le Moyne left France for England; most probably they were made about 1568, shortly after his return to France from Laudonnière's expedition to Florida, on which he had been employed as recording artist. Le Moyne combined an intensity of vision with an ability to express form, colour and texture with microscopic exactness. Botanical illustrations like these met the demand of educated men who were inquisitive about the natural world and anxious to examine it in detail.

Bibl: P.H. Hulton, *The Work of Jacques Le Moyne de Morgues; a Hugenot artist working in France, Florida and England*, 1977, I, pp. 155-162, II, pl. 28b.

93. Thomas Chippendale (*c.* 1718-1779);
British
A desk and bookcase. Design for a bureau
bookcase with the interior fitting of the desk
shown below, a drawing for plate III in the
Gentleman and Cabinet-Maker's Director by
Thomas Chippendale, third edition
published London, 1762
Signed *T.Chippendale*.
Inscribed with title, dimensions of bookcase,
Pl 111 and *Darly Sculp*
Pen and ink and wash on laid paper
31.7 x 14.1 cm.
The drawing was engraved for Chippendale
by Matthew Darly (worked *c.* 1750-1778).
The publication of engraved plates of
designs for furniture and fittings played an
increasingly important role in furniture
production from the 1740s. The first edition
of the *Director* was published in 1754, and of
all the many pattern books published, it was
and has remained the most popular, influential and comprehensive. It was, moreover,
the first to be devoted solely to furniture,
and to provide a complete range of designs
in the 'Chippendale style' from which
patrons could make selections and through
which craftsmen could find guidance and
inspiration for their work. A second edition
followed in 1755, and a third in 1762, the
latter marked by certain omissions and
additions which reflected minor changes in
taste over the period.

94. John Sell Cotman (1782-1842); British Church of St. Michel, Vaucelles near Bayeux: exterior from south-west. Drawing for Plate 18 of *Architectural Antiquities of Normandy* by Dawson Turner, illustrated by J.S. Cotman, published in two volumes in London, 1822.
Signed in pencil *J.S.Cotman.*
Inscribed *Sketched July 24th 1817. Tour de l'eglise de St Michel dans le fauxbourg de vaucelles a Caen*
Pencil and wash. 33.6 x 23.5 cm.
Dawson Turner (1775-1858) was a banker, botanist and antiquarian who became both patron and friend to Cotman. Cotman had the example of Turner's visit to Normandy in 1815 to inspire him to make the first of his three visits there in 1817, a trip which he planned to satisfy his own curiosity about the possible Norman antecedents of Norfolk architecture. Many of the drawings made on Cotman's Normandy tours were executed with the help of a *camera lucida*, a mechanical aid to drawing in perspective much used by topographical draughtsmen at the time, and admirable for the literal transcripts demanded by antiquarian studies. Cotman contributed many illustrations to Dawson Turner's *Account of a Tour in Normandy*, published in two volumes, London, 1820, as well as all those for *Architectural Antiquities of Normandy*, published two years later.

95. Anonymous; possibly Belgian or Swiss
Two sheets with designs for cups from a
trade pattern book with 113 sheets of
designs for vases, table-ware, etc. Possibly
for a Belgian or Swiss Factory. *c.* 1820
Inscribed in French on one sheet, and on
small labels stuck on the other, with notes,
numbers and prices of individual designs.
Pen and ink and water- and body-colour
Size of sheets 32.7 x 51.4 cm.
The drawings, which record the variety of
decorative patterns within a range of basic
shapes, may well have been made for the
factory by the painter who decorated the
original pottery. These records of the
designs would be useful as a catalogue of
available wares. See Plate XXVI.

D. 1545-1901

96. Possibly by Thomas Grieve (1799-1882);
British
Drawing recording properties used in
Charles Kean's production of Shakespeare's
The Winter's Tale, first produced at the
Princess's Theatre, London, 28 April 1856
Each property inscribed with a letter
referring to a key
Water- and body-colour and pencil.
Size of sheet 17.4 x 24.4 cm.
The original scenery for this production of
The Winter's Tale was painted under the
direction of Thomas Grieve. The drawing is
one of many record copies made for Kean
after designs for scenery and properties by
various artists, which were used in his
productions from 1848 to 1859. For Kean
everything had to be solid, accurate and
archeologically exact, and these productions
were the culmination of the nineteenth-
century swing towards representational
scene design.

97. Manwaring Shurlock; British
Copy of thirteenth century encaustic tiles
found during excavations at Chertsey
Abbey, Surrey in 1861. Four sections of
frame tiles, two bordered with grotesques
and two with fragments of an inscription
from an early Romance poem, *Sir Tristrem*.
Water-colour. 40.6 x 39.9 cm.
The water-colour is varnished to resemble
the surface appearance of an encaustic tile.

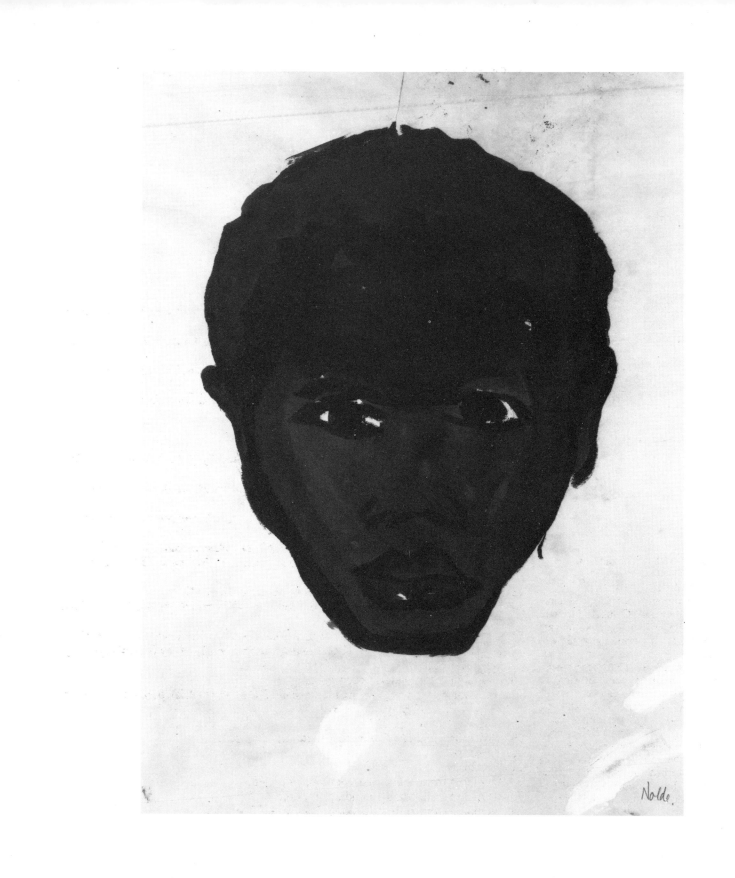

NOTES

98. Emil Nolde (1867-1956); German
Negro Head. 1913-14
Signed in pencil *Nolde*
Water-colour on Japan paper. 47 x 34.8 cm.
In 1913-14 the German Colonial Ministry
organised an expedition to investigate
standards of health in German new Guinea
and invited Nolde to take part in the
expedition as the official pictorial reporter.
During the trip he made many drawings of
the tropical landscape and plant life but he
was particularly attracted to the natives,
believing them to represent man in a
primordial state: this is one of the many
studies he made. While the pretext for the
execution of the drawing was Nolde's
commission to record the expedition, such
images were to be an important source of
inspiration for his paintings in the years to
come.

1. pp. 1-2.
2. Quoted from J. Meder, *The Mastery of Drawing*, trans. and rev. by W. Ames, 1978, I, pp. 19-20.
3. Cennino Cennini, *A Practical Treatise on Painting in Fresco, Oil and Distemper*, trans. M.P. Merrifield, 1844, p. 9.
4. G. Vasari, *The Lives of the Painters, Sculptors and Architects*, Everyman's ed., 1963, 111, p. 188.
5. Quoted from H. Delaborde, *Ingres, Sa Vie, Ses Travaux, Sa Doctrine*, 1870, p. 123.
6. Cennini, op. cit., p. 63.
7. Vasari, op. cit., II, p. 208.
8. Leonardo da Vinci, *Treatise on Painting*, trans. by A.P. MacMahon, 1956, p. 45.
9. Quoted from H.C. Hutchinson, *The History of the Royal Academy 1768-1968*, p. 48.
10. Quoted from Mrs. Bray, *Life of Thomas Stothard, RA, with personal reminiscences*, 1851, p. 78.
11. Quoted from W.P. Frith, *My Autobiography and Reminiscences*, 1851, p. 78.
12. *Racontars de Rapin*, 1902; quoted from trans. in R. Pickvance, *The Drawings of Gauguin*, p. 5.
13. *The Complete Letters of Vincent Van Gogh*, 1958, II, p. 317.
14. *Bauhaus*, 2/3, p. 10-11; quoted from trans. in exhib. cat., Royal Academy of Arts, *50 Years Bauhaus*, 1968, p. 52.
15. P. Klee, 'Wege des Naturstudiums', *Staatliches Bauhaus*, Wiemar, 1919-1923; quoted from trans. in P. Klee, *Pedagogical Sketchbook*, ed. by S. Moholy-Nagy, 1953, p. 12.
16. Quoted from Meder, op. cit., p. 35.
17. C. Malvasia, *Felsina Pittrice; Vite de Pittori Bolognesi*, 1678, III, p. 184, quoted from trans. in Meder, op. cit., p. 319.
18. Meder, op. cit., p. 162.
19. M. Cormack, *The Drawings of Watteau*, 1970, p. 5.
20. Ibid, p. 5.
21. p. 28.
22. Quoted from trans. in Meder, op. cit., p. 282.
23. Quoted from trans. in ibid., p. 15, note 2.
24. Quoted from J. Rewald, *Paul Cézanne*, 1950, p. 160.

SUGGESTIONS FOR FURTHER READING

There are many books on drawing treating the subject from a variety of angles including by artist, period and genre. No attempt has been made to provide full bibliographies for each of the drawings reproduced but the captions include the fullest or most recent reference which will lead the interested reader to additional bibliographical references. The abbreviations Ward-Jackson I and II refer to the Victoria & Albert Museum Catalogues by P. Ward-Jackson, *Italian Drawings, volume one: 14th-16th century*, 1979 and *volume two: 17th-18th century*, 1980. Lugt refers to F. Lugt, *Les marques de collections de dessins et d'estampes ... avec des notices historiques sur les collectioneurs, les collections, les ventes, les marchands et editeurs*, Amsterdam, 1921.

The following general books are particularly helpful on the aspects discussed here:

C. Ashwin, *Encyclopaedia of drawing material, technique and style*, 1982
H. Hutter, *Drawing: history and technique*, 1968
J. Meder, *The mastery of drawing*, trans. and rev. by Winslow Ames, 1978
P. Rawson, *Drawing*, 1969
J. Watrous, *The craft of old-master drawings*, 1957
Welsh Arts Council, K. Baynes and F. Pugh, *The art of the engineer. Two hundred years in the development of drawings for design of transport on land, sea and air*, 1978

Acknowledgments

Almost everyone in the Department of Prints, Drawings & Photographs and Paintings at the Victoria & Albert Museum has been involved in some way in the production of this book or in the organisation of the exhibition which it accompanies and I should like to thank them all. I am particularly grateful to Margaret Timmers and Michael Snodin who contributed many of the entries in the 1981 exhibition catalogue from which this book has evolved and to Sally Chappell of the Photographic Studio for taking many of the black and white photographs.

Index to illustrations

OTHER PANTHEON TITLES OF INTEREST

About Looking by John Berger
Paperbound, $4.95
0-394-73907-8

The American Image: Photographs from the National Archives, 1860-1960 by
the National Archives Trust Fund Board
Paperbound, $10.00
0-394-73815-2

Another Way of Telling by John Berger
Paperbound, $9.95
0-394-73998-1

How Pictures Mean by Hans Hess
Paperbound, $6.95
0-394-73057-7

Images of Revolution: Graphic Art from 1905 Russia by David King and Cathy Porter
Paperbound, $16.95
0-394-72199-3

Overlay: Contemporary Art and the Art of Prehistory by Lucy Lippard
Paperbound, $16.95
0-394-71145-9

Reading Photographs: Understanding the Aesthetics of Photography by
The Photographers' Gallery and Jonathan Bayer
Paperbound, $9.95
0-394-73584-6